1918
HOW THE
FIRST WORLD WAR
WAS WON

THIS IS AN ANDRE DEUTSCH BOOK

First published in 2018
by André Deutsch Limited,
a division of the Carlton Publishing Group,
20 Mortimer Street, London W1T 3JW

Text copyright © Julian Thompson 2018

Design copyright © André Deutsch Limited 2018

Maps by Martin Lubikowski, ML Design, London 2018

Imperial War Museum photographs © Imperial War Museums 2018

Printed in Dubai

A CIP catalogue for this book is available from the British Library

ISBN: 978 0 233 00557 7

JULIAN THOMPSON

1918
HOW THE
FIRST WORLD WAR
WAS WON

IN PARTNERSHIP WITH
IMPERIAL WAR MUSEUMS

ANDRE
DEUTSCH

CONTENTS

INTRODUCTION 8

PART 1 — THE GERMANS MOVE 12

1   THE TREATY OF BREST-LITOVSK 14

2   THE GERMAN MARCH OFFENSIVE — OPERATION MICHAEL 20

3   THE GERMAN APRIL OFFENSIVE — OPERATION GEORGETTE, THE BATTLE OF THE LYS 28

4   THE GERMAN MAY/JUNE OFFENSIVES 36

PART 2 — WAR IN THE AIR AND AT SEA 46

5   ZEEBRUGGE, 23 APRIL 1918 48

6   THE WAR AT SEA 56

7   THE WAR IN THE AIR 64

PART 3 — OTHER FRONTS 70

8   THE BATTLE OF THE PIAVE, ITALY 72

9   THE TURKISH FRONTS IN THE MIDDLE EAST 80

PART 4 — OVERTURE TO CHANGING FORTUNES 88

10   NEW BRITISH TACTICS 90

11   THE SECOND BATTLE OF THE MARNE 96

12   LE HAMEL 104

13   THE ALLIES PLAN TO ROLL THE GERMANS BACK 110

PART 5 — THE BATTLE OF AMIENS 116

14   PREPARING 118

15   FIRST DAY — BRITISH III CORPS 124

16   FIRST DAY — AUSTRALIAN CORPS 132

17   FIRST DAY — CANADIAN CORPS 138

18	9 TO 11 AUGUST	142
19	BATTLE OF ST MIHIEL	148
	PART 6 — OTHER FRONTS	158
20	THE MIDDLE EAST — THE BATTLE OF MEGIDDO	160
21	THE BALKANS	168
22	ITALY, THE BATTLE OF VITTORIO VENETO	176
	PART 7 — CONTINUING THE ADVANCE ON THE WESTERN FRONT	182
23	BATTLES OF ALBERT/SCARPE	184
24	MEUSE/ARGONNE — FRENCH AND AMERICANS	190
	PART 8 — FINAL BATTLES	198
25	CANAL DU NORD AND FLANDERS	200
26	BREACHING THE HINDENBURG LINE	206
27	CROSSING THE ST QUENTIN CANAL	212
28	CHAMPAGNE AND BLANC MONT	216
29	ALLIED ALLIANCE — CAMBRAI AND LE CATEAU	222
	PART 9 — AN END TO WAR	228
30	ALLIED ALLIANCE — LILLE, SELLE AND SAMBRE	230
31	ARMISTICE	236
32	VERSAILLES	242
	GLOSSARY	250
	INDEX	252
	CREDITS	256

INTRODUCTION

AS 1918 BEGAN IT USHERED IN THE FIFTH YEAR OF A WAR THAT
MANY HAD PROPHESIZED WOULD BE OVER BY CHRISTMAS 1914.
THE NEW YEAR BROUGHT LITTLE COMFORT FOR THE ENTENTE ALLIES
(FRANCE, BRITAIN, RUSSIA, SERBIA, AMERICA AND ITALY).

Russia, now the world's first communist state, was effectively out of the war, and would soon be neutral. The German Chief of Staff on the Eastern front described Russia as "no more than a vast heap of maggots". The United States had entered the contest eight months previously with much euphoria amongst the Allies, but apart from volunteers in foreign armies and air forces, few Americans had seen action. General John Pershing, the Commander-in-Chief of the American Expeditionary Force, forecast that he would have 120–150,000 men in France by 1 January 1918, and half a million by the end of that year. Recruiting large numbers of men is merely the beginning of forming an effective army from a small cadre of regulars – the situation in America in 1917. An army has to be trained and equipped, formed into regiments, divisions, and corps. The staffs for these hitherto non-existent formations have to be selected and trained. At every level, amateurs have to be turned into professionals – a time-consuming process. The British Prime Minister, David Lloyd George, noted in his war memoirs: "When the Armistice was signed on November 11th, half the aeroplanes used by the American Army were of French or British make … No field guns of American pattern or manufacture fired a shot in the War. The same applied to tanks."

Until 1917 the French Army had borne by far the greatest share of fighting on the Western Front. The breaking point was almost reached after the failure of General Robert Nivelle's offensive in April 1917. Much had been promised, including significant success within 48 hours from a supposedly war-winning formula. When it turned into yet another battle of attrition, the disappointment was devastating. The result was much discontent in the French Army. Some 110 regiments in 54 divisions on the Western Front were affected. The symptoms ranged from refusing to participate in any more attacks, to full-scale mutiny. Soldiers on leave joined workers in strikes. The French were weary and longed for peace. The mutinies were not in opposition to the struggle to defeat Germany, which occupied such a large area of France's key industrial region. They were a protest against the treatment endured by the soldiers, including appallingly bad administration, insufficient leave, disgracefully inadequate medical facilities and futile attacks with insufficient artillery support. The new Commander-in-Chief, General Philippe Pétain, regained their confidence by his demonstrable care for their administration, his well-prepared operations at Verdun in August 1917 and on the Chemin des Dames in October.

The gloom was finally dispelled when 76-year-old Georges Clemenceau, the "Tiger", became Prime Minister of France on 16 November. Winston Churchill watched his speech to the Chamber of Deputies:

Previous page: Field Marshal Sir Douglas Haig (left) and President Clemenceau inspect a French guard of honour in October 1918. Haig and Clemenceau quickly established a rapport.

Left: General Sir William Robertson (left), the British Chief of the Imperial General Staff, and Marshal Ferdinand Foch.

BRITISH PRIME MINISTER, DAVID LLOYD GEORGE

David Lloyd George, known as the "Welsh Wizard", practised as a solicitor before entering parliament as a Liberal MP in 1890, retaining his seat until 1945. After holding several ministerial posts, he became Prime Minister in December 1916, with Conservative backing, promising "a more vigorous prosecution of the war". His relations with senior British commanders, especially Haig (Commander-in-Chief, British Expeditionary Force) and Robertson (CIGS) were strained, and not helped by his advocacy of the concept of "knocking away the props" in the belief that Germany would then collapse. This involved suggestions for attacking Germany's allies anywhere other than on the Western Front, and included schemes that were pure fantasy, such as attacking up the Danube, and an offensive in Macedonia. Although he wanted to replace Haig, he was unable to do so. He did manage to sack Robertson, replacing him with the devious Henry Wilson. He was totally taken in by the flamboyant and articulate French general Nivelle, even placing Haig under his command for a short period – until Nivelle was sacked when his promises came to naught.

Lloyd George's memoirs, written after most of his senior generals had died (most notably Haig) were a flagrant self-vindication of his conduct of the war. He depicted himself as blameless for any of the controversial decisions: it was all the fault of the generals. He is still remembered as a brilliant politician.

"He looked like a wild animal pacing to and fro … With snarls and growls, the ferocious, aged, dauntless beast of prey went into action."

On the Italian front, 1917 had seen disaster after disaster, culminating in the battle of Caporetto in October. With the help of 11 British and French divisions, the Italians managed to halt the Austrian/German advance on the Piave. The Allies met at Rapallo to discuss the situation, and on 5 November 1917 decided to set up a Supreme War Council, and eventually appointed General Ferdinand Foch as Allied Supreme Commander on the Western Front. It would be incorrect to picture Foch as equivalent to Eisenhower in the Second World War. He was a coordinator, operated with a small staff, and could only advise and persuade his fellow Allied generals, rather than order them to carry out his wishes.

The British Expeditionary Force (BEF) meanwhile was saddled with cuts to its strength instigated by the mendacious Lloyd George. In essence these affected the infantry and every division was reduced from 12 infantry battalions in each division to nine. So while the Germans were preparing for an offensive, the BEF was reorganizing and losing 141 infantry battalions in the process. Fortunately the Australian, Canadian and New Zealand governments refused to follow suit, and retained 12 infantry battalion divisions.

At sea the Allies were getting the measure of the U-boat menace thanks to the introduction of convoys in April 1917.

By 1917 Germany was suffering from severe shortages of food, mainly as a result of the highly effective blockade by the British Royal Navy. The result was strikes and unrest, beginning in the industrial heartland, the Ruhr. In 1918, workers in key munitions factories in Hamburg, Berlin, Essen and Leipzig went on strike, accompanied by acts of sabotage and rioting. For lack of maintenance, the railways began to break down, which resulted in coal shortages. Field Marshal Hindenburg ran the country almost as a military dictatorship. But he was really a figurehead: the brilliant but unstable Ludendorff provided the brains and direction. These two were to instigate the moves that were to dominate events on the Western Front in the opening months of 1918.

FIELD MARSHAL PAUL VON HINDENBURG

After serving as a junior officer in the Prussian Guard in the wars leading to the unification of Germany, Hindenburg retired in 1911 as a corps commander. In 1914, he was recalled to command the German Army in East Prussia, which was retreating before the Russian offensive. With Ludendorff as his Chief of Staff, he won smashing victories at Tannenberg and the Masurian Lakes. His name was now synonymous with victory. He retained this reputation over the next two years as Commander-in-Chief of the Eastern Front. In August 1916 he replaced Erich von Falkenhayn as Chief of the Imperial German General Staff with Ludendorff as his deputy. He was out of his depth at this level. He supported the policy of unrestricted submarine warfare, which was largely responsible for America joining the Entente Allies. He allowed Ludendorff to fritter away the manpower of the German Army on the 1918 March and April offensives. Finally, with defeat staring Germany in the face in late 1918, he remained in office to see his country through the turmoil that ensued. From 1925 he served as President of the Weimar Republic, in which capacity he appointed Adolf Hitler as German Chancellor in 1933. He remained a national hero until his death in 1934. Hindenburg is on the left of the picture below, with the Kaiser in the centre, and Ludendorff on the right.

PART 1
THE GERMANS MOVE

THE TREATY OF BREST-LITOVSK

THE BOLSHEVIKS SEIZED POWER IN RUSSIA ON 7 NOVEMBER 1917 (26 OCTOBER BY THE RUSSIAN CALENDAR). AS PROMISED IN THEIR PROPAGANDA, THEY IMMEDIATELY SUED FOR AN ARMISTICE WITH GERMANY AND AUSTRIA-HUNGARY, AND FIGHTING ON THE EASTERN FRONT CEASED ON 28 NOVEMBER.

Negotiations began at Brest-Litovsk on 22 December 1917. Sir John Wheeler-Bennett, historian of the negotiations, wrote: "The whim of history willed that representatives of the most revolutionary regime ever known should sit at the diplomatic table with the representatives of the most reactionary military caste among all ruling classes." The parleying lasted 10 weeks during which all the Bolshevik fantasies were demolished as they were reminded of the enduring principle: might is right. Whimsical left-wing notions of peace and man's humanity to man as the natural order of things were melted away by the intense desire of Germany to dispose of the Russians before the American Army was properly organized and battle-ready.

To begin with, the Bolshevik delegates, led by Leon Trotsky, refused the harsh terms on offer, hoping that world opinion, and especially "the masses" in Germany and Austria-Hungary, would support them. A believer in the theory of permanent revolution, Trotsky attempted to gain time to allow the workers' revolution in Germany and the rest of Europe to come about. On 18 February 1918, the Germans gave their answer. Their armies struck, advancing 150 miles in five days against pathetic opposition. Capturing Kiev and Odessa, and occupying

the Ukraine, Livonia and Estonia, the Germans were within 150 miles of Petrograd (the Russian capital). Ever the pragmatist, Vladimir Lenin finally perceived that if the delegates did not sign the terms of the treaty on offer, the Central Powers, concluding that the Bolsheviks were not going to deliver, would press on to occupy Petrograd and Moscow. That would have been the end of the Bolshevik revolution. By a vote of seven to four with

Previous page: *German storm troopers advancing through smoke.*

Left: *Map showing territory ceded by Russia to Germany. The "self determined areas" were swiftly occupied by Germany as well as the region shown in red. From George H. Allen:* The Great War,

Volume 5: The Triumph of Democracy. *George Barrie's Sons, Philadelphia 1921.*

Above: *German troops occupy Kiev, 1 March 1918.*

another four abstentions, the Russians agreed to sign. Neither Lenin nor Trotsky were present: Lenin because he did not want the stigma; Trotsky because he wanted to keep the process in play. On 3 March the Treaty of Brest-Litovsk was signed. Grigori Sokolnikov carried out the unenviable task, which no other party in Russia approved.

The Bolsheviks had gained power by promising the end of the war. Now came the "bill": Russia lost 34 per cent of her population, 32 per cent of her agricultural land, 85 per cent of her beet-sugar land, 54 per cent of her industrial capacity, and 89 per cent of her coal mines. The German government announced that they had worked only for a peace of understanding and conciliation. The Bolshevik delegate Sokolnikov called it "a peace which

Russia, grinding its teeth, is forced to accept". Wheeler-Bennett wrote: "the peace of Brest-Litovsk … showed clearly to the world what mercy the conquered enemies of Germany might expect. The effect in the Allied countries was a grim tightening of the belt and an increased determination to destroy the regime that could make such a peace." The terms imposed at Brest-Litovsk made utter

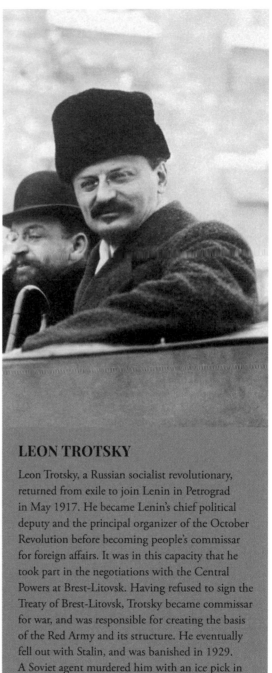

LEON TROTSKY

Leon Trotsky, a Russian socialist revolutionary, returned from exile to join Lenin in Petrograd in May 1917. He became Lenin's chief political deputy and the principal organizer of the October Revolution before becoming people's commissar for foreign affairs. It was in this capacity that he took part in the negotiations with the Central Powers at Brest-Litovsk. Having refused to sign the Treaty of Brest-Litovsk, Trotsky became commissar for war, and was responsible for creating the basis of the Red Army and its structure. He eventually fell out with Stalin, and was banished in 1929. A Soviet agent murdered him with an ice pick in Mexico on 20 August 1940.

Left: *Leon Trotsky arrives at Brest-Litovsk, 1918.*

nonsense of the notion, championed by some at the time, and which persists in some quarters to this day, that peace with Germany could be negotiated while they were still in possession of large tracts of other people's countries. Furthermore, these terms, imposed by an expansionist and ruthless Germany, provide demonstrable proof that the First World War was not, as is so often asserted, futile. Germany's motivation for going to war in 1914 was in large part driven by a yearning for territorial gain – as it was again in 1939. Adolf Hitler would call it *Lebensraum* or "living space" – his reason for invading the Soviet Union in 1941.

The terms of the treaty also came with a "bill" for Germany. Part of the reason for demanding so much Russian territory was to recreate ancient Germanic kingdoms and grand-duchies – an aspiration strongly supported by Erich von Ludendorff. Germany expanded

into Finland, and sent forces into the oil-fields of Batoum and Baku, and also into Odessa to occupy the Ukraine and Romania. To maintain a hold on these demanded troops. All this meant that a million German soldiers were kept in the east, when Ludendorff knew perfectly well that every man was needed to implement his plans for the Western Front.

Despite this error of judgement on Ludendorff's part, the buildup of German strength in the west was alarming, and well known to Intelligence staff at General Headquarters (GHQ) of the British Expeditionary Force (BEF). In November 1917 there were around 150 German divisions on the Western Front opposing the Allies there. By the end of December there were 171. As the Germans moved divisions west, GHQ Intelligence spotted their presence within a few days. By 21 March 1918 the figure was 192, eventually rising to 208 divisions.

Below: *German troops examining an armoured car captured from the Bolsheviks. Kiev, March 1918.*

GENERAL ERICH VON LUDENDORFF

An abrasive and violent officer to the point of being mentally unstable, and an advocate of total war, Ludendorff's career prospects really took off in 1914 as the Deputy Chief of Staff in the Second Army in Belgium. He took command of a brigade when the siege of Liège was locked in stalemate and succeeded in breaking through the ring of fortresses, leading to the fall of the city. He was sent to be Chief of Staff of the Eighth Army on the Eastern Front under Paul von Hindenburg. His success there resulted in him accompanying Hindenburg when the latter assumed supreme command of the army. Together, Hindenburg and Ludendorff effectively dictated all German strategic decisions. Soon Hindenburg allowed Ludendorff to become commander of the army in all but name, with considerable influence on how Germany conducted the war.

Ludendorff's strategic vision was flawed, with perhaps the best example being the 1918 offensives. Had he not carried these out, it is possible that he would have forced Western powers to do the attacking if they intended to win the war. This might have been more than they could bear after the disappointments of 1916 and 1917. The German defences were formidable, and so far had proved too hard a nut to crack to the point of breaking open completely. But there were internal pressures on Ludendorff and Hindenburg, consisting of strikes and unrest among the workers and the ultra-left in Germany, and talk in Austria hinting at making a separate peace. All this inclined them to risk going for broke, opting for a "win or bust" strategy.

Above: *Kaiser Wilhelm II (centre) studying operational maps with Field Marshal Paul von Hindenburg (left) and General Erich von Ludendorff (right). Hindenburg, who replaced Erich von Falkenhayn as the Chief of the German General Staff on 29 August, acted mainly as a figurehead, allowing Ludendorff to shape much of Germany's military policy.*

2

GERMAN SPRING OFFENSIVES 1918

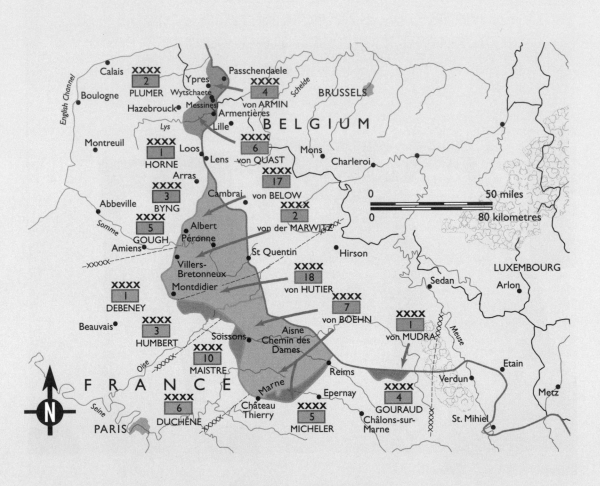

German gains from Operations:
- Michael, 21 March–5 April
- Georgette, 9–11 April
- Blücher-Yorck, 27 May
- Gneisenau, 9 June
- Marne-Reims, 15–17 July

THE GERMAN MARCH OFFENSIVE – OPERATION MICHAEL

AT 4.40 AM ON 21 MARCH, OVER 6,000 GERMAN GUNS AND 3,500 MORTARS BEGAN A MASSIVE BOMBARDMENT ON THE SECTOR OF THE WESTERN FRONT HELD BY GENERAL SIR HUBERT GOUGH'S BRITISH FIFTH ARMY, AND GENERAL SIR JULIAN BYNG'S BRITISH THIRD ARMY.

The hurricane of fire devastated great stretches of the British defence line along 42 miles of the front. In some places, according to the British Official History, "the troops occupying the Forward Zone had been mostly killed, buried by the bombardment, or taken prisoner, the few survivors were not capable of much resistance, and none returned to tell the tale."

After five hours of remorseless pounding, the bombardment lifted, and German infantry swarmed over in the thick fog blanketing the Third and Fifth Army front. The British line was breached. This was the *Kaiserschlacht* (the Emperor's Battle – Operation Michael after the patron saint of Germany), an attack by three German armies, Eighteenth, Second and Seventeenth, consisting of 71 divisions; their aim: to force a wedge between the British and French Armies. The Germans believed that the French would be concerned with protecting Paris, whereas the British would be anxious to safeguard their line of communication to the Channel ports. The Germans calculated that in a dire situation these conflicting priorities would result in the Allies withdrawing in different directions: the French south-west, and the British north-west – ripping open the front.

Left: *Map of the spring offensive.*

Above: *German infantry climbing out of a trench or shell hole – possibly during a rehearsal.*

LIEUTENANT GENERAL SIR HUBERT GOUGH

A cavalryman who acquired a reputation for dash in South Africa in the Second Boer War, by 1911 Gough was commanding a cavalry brigade at the Curragh in Ireland. In March 1914, fearful that the army would be used to compel Ulster into a united Ireland, Gough resigned, as did most of his officers. Summoned to London, he secured a promise that opposition to Irish home rule would not be suppressed. The British government repudiated this undertaking, and John Seely, the Secretary of State for War, and the Chief of the Imperial General Staff, Field Marshal Sir John French, were obliged to resign. Notwithstanding this, Gough took his brigade to France in 1914, and rose rapidly: command of 2nd Cavalry Division in the autumn, corps command by mid 1915, and Fifth Army in 1916. His command style did not stand him in good stead at the Third Battle of Ypres in Autumn 1917. Early 1918 found his army at the southern end of the British portion of the front. He pointed out that he was short of troops, that the French positions he had taken over were badly constructed, and that all the signs were that the Germans were about to attack in

force. When, as forecast, the Germans did attack and his army was hurled back with heavy losses, Gough was replaced by Henry Rawlinson. Gough was made the scapegoat, as Douglas Haig was later to admit. But Gough's arrogant and hot-tempered manner made him few friends, and many people were glad to see him go.

Along with the rest of the BEF, the Fifth Army was understrength, thanks to David Lloyd George holding back replacement troops (see Introduction), and overstretched having only recently taken over ground from the French left flank around St Quentin. In this sector, the German Eighteenth Army broke through in and, by crossing the 1916 Somme battlefields, threatened Amiens. Initially the British Third Army fared better, and the German Seventeenth and Second Armies' gains were limited.

On 24 March, Field Marshal Sir Douglas Haig, having asked General Philippe Pétain for assistance, learned that Pétain was under orders from his government to cover Paris at all costs, so no help would be forthcoming from him. This impelled Haig to persuade both the British and French governments at a meeting at Doullens on 25 March, to appoint General Ferdinand Foch to coordinate the action of all the Allied Armies on the Western Front. Duly

appointed on 26 March, Foch was to remain in this post until the end of the war.

Meanwhile the German advance began to peter out. On 5 April, Ludendorff halted his March offensive a mere nine miles from Amiens, an advance of some 40 miles – further than anyone had achieved on the Western Front since stalemate had set in 40 months earlier in November 1914. The Allies had lost ground, paid for in much blood in the Somme battles of 1916. Now they had suffered nearly a quarter of a million casualties – the British at 178,000 casualties, including over 70,000 prisoners, and the French at 77,000. German losses totalled about the same as the Allies'. But the Germans did not achieve the hoped for breakthrough leading to ultimate victory. Why did the German offensive fail?

Ludendorff divided his divisions into shock troops, attack troops and follow-up formations. The most

OPERATION MICHAEL, 21 MARCH–4 APRIL 1918

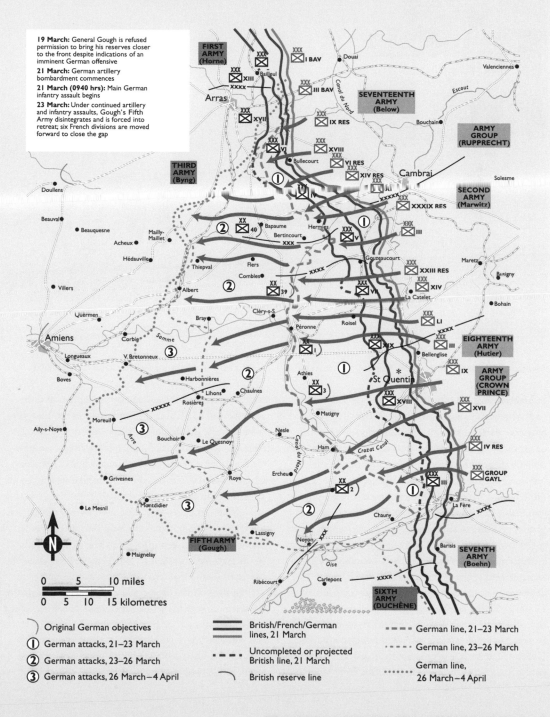

19 March: General Gough is refused permission to bring his reserves closer to the front despite indications of an imminent German offensive

21 March: German artillery bombardment commences

21 March (0940 hrs): Main German infantry assault begins

23 March: Under continued artillery and infantry assaults, Gough's Fifth Army disintegrates and is forced into retreat; six French divisions are moved forward to close the gap

FIRST ARMY (Horne)

Douai

Valenciennes

Bailleul

I BAV

XIII

III BAV

Arras

SEVENTEENTH ARMY (Below)

Canal du Nord

Escout

Bouchain

XVII

IX RES

ARMY GROUP (RUPPRECHT)

VI

XVIII

Bullecourt

VI RES

XIV RES

Cambrai

Solesme

THIRD ARMY (Byng)

Doullens

Beauval

Beauquesne

Acheux

Mailly-Maillet

Hédauville

40

Bapaume

Bertincourt

Hermies

V

III

SECOND ARMY (Marwitz)

XXXIX RES

Thiepval

Flers

Combles

Gouzeaucourt

XXIII RES

Maretz

Busigny

Villers

Albert

39

La Catelet

XIV

Bohain

Quérmen

Bray

Cléry-s-S

Péronne

Roisel

LI

Amiens

Corbie

Somme

I

XIX

Bellenglise

III

EIGHTEENTH ARMY (Hutier)

Longueaux

V. Bretonneux

Athies

St Quentin

IX

ARMY GROUP (CROWN PRINCE)

Boves

Harbonnières

3

Chaulnes

XVII

Lihons

Rosières

Matigny

Aily-s-Noye

Moreuil

Bouchoir

Le Quesnoy

Nesle

Ham

Crozat Canal

IV RES

Grivesnes

Royè

Ercheu

2

GROUP GAYL

III

La Fère

Le Mesnil

Montdidier

Chauny

Barisis

Lassigny

Noyon

SEVENTH ARMY (Boehn)

Maignelay

FIFTH ARMY (Gough)

Oise

Ribécourt

Carlepont

SIXTH ARMY (DUCHÊNE)

N

0   5   10 miles

0   5   10   15 kilometres

) Original German objectives

① German attacks, 21–23 March

② German attacks, 23–26 March

③ German attacks, 26 March–4 April

British/French/German lines, 21 March

Uncompleted or projected British line, 21 March

British reserve line

--- German line, 21–23 March

--- German line, 23–26 March

···· German line, 26 March–4 April

Above: *A British Mark IV tank near Péronne.*

Right: *German infantry supported by a German A7V tank.*

skilled were formed into storm troops. These were not to attack in lines, but to penetrate British defences wherever there were opportunities to do so, bypassing any resistance, and leaving follow-up troops to eliminate these. Ludendorff's artillery would not keep up the bombardment for days as had happened in the past, but having deluged the rear areas, headquarters and gun lines, would switch to the defence zones in a short hurricane of fire to stun the defenders just in advance of the storm troop assault. Many historians have expressed admiration for these tactics. Others, including the author, believe they were deeply flawed. The major deficiency was the inability to get the German artillery forward speedily. Ludendorff was gambling on the fact that after their initial success, the storm troopers would be able to prevail on their own, without artillery support. Unless the defenders were so disorganized as to be almost non-effective, this tactic would fail. The storm troop

tactic was only effective in the opening phase of each successive attack. Casualties among the storm troopers were heavy, and while the artillery was striving to get forward, the infantry had only relatively light weapons for fire support. The defenders meanwhile could move up guns and reserves and slow the impetus of the attack, eventually bringing it to a complete stop.

Ludendorff's other error, besides unsound tactics, was leaving around a million troops on the Eastern Front, for reasons covered in an earlier chapter. Half this number would have been more than sufficient, had Ludendorff restricted them to occupying duties; another half a million men on the Western Front might have turned the balance in favour of the Germans. Ludendorff was guilty of the "military sin" of having two aims: expansion in the east while trying to win the war in the west. Four days after ending Operation Michael, Ludendorff attacked again, in Flanders, employing the same tactics.

FIELD MARSHAL
SIR DOUGLAS HAIG

Haig commanded I Corps in the 1914 BEF and the
First Army after the new command level of army was
created. He became Commander-in-Chief of the BEF
on 19 December 1915, succeeding Field Marshal
Sir John French. Haig's impassive demeanour and
curt delivery did not impress Lloyd George who, like
some of Haig's critics, thought that this showed that
Haig was dull-witted. He was in reality an intelligent,
professional soldier with a questioning mind, and
contrary to popular myth, an enthusiastic supporter
of the tank, machine gun, aircraft and indeed any
idea or equipment that he thought would help win
the war. He visited troops almost every day and was
interested in the views of the most junior ranks.

GENERAL PHILIPPE PÉTAIN

Pétain was the son of a peasant from Pas-de-Calais and in 1914 an infantry colonel with no expectations of promotion. Two years later he became the saviour of Verdun and France. In 1917, he was called upon to save France again when the French Army mutinied. Pétain was sent for, and as well as dealing with the ringleaders, he introduced numerous reforms which improved the conditions of the soldiers: regular leave, reliable leave trains, well-stocked canteens behind the lines and improved food. He spoke plainly to his soldiers and was trusted by them. After the war he was promoted to Marshal. Despite his outwardly cold demeanour, some women found him attractive. An Anglophobe, he did not trouble to conceal his loathing of politicians. French Prime Minister Georges Clemenceau judged that he could be defeatist. In 1940 Clemenceau was proved right.

Right: *German artillery following up the advancing infantry over the first captured British trenches west of St Quentin.*

3

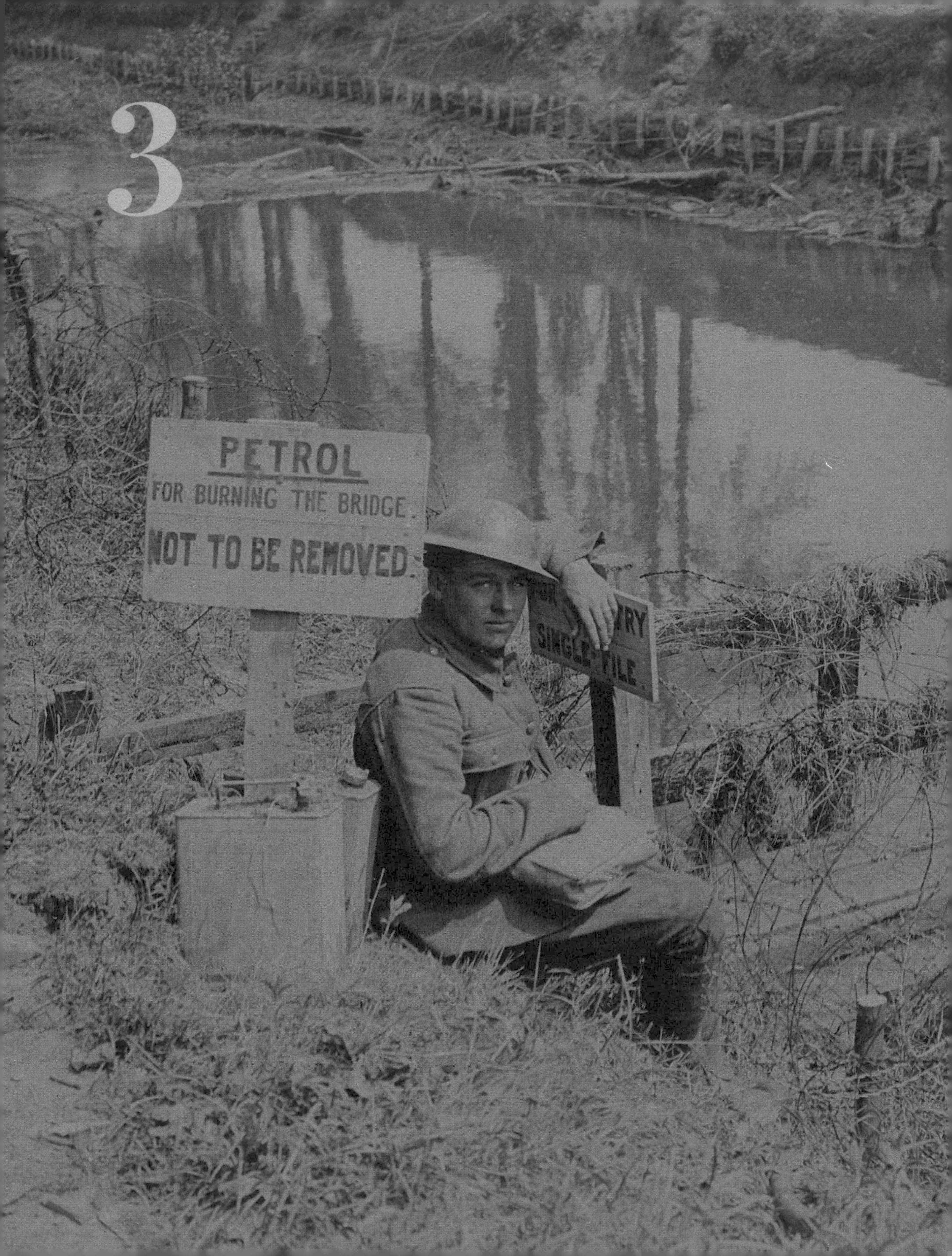

THE GERMAN APRIL OFFENSIVE – OPERATION GEORGETTE, THE BATTLE OF THE LYS

AT 4.00 AM ON 9 APRIL, THE GERMAN SIXTH ARMY ATTACKED WITH 17 DIVISIONS BETWEEN ARMENTIÈRES AND BÉTHUNE ASTRIDE THE RIVER LYS – HENCE THE BRITISH NAME FOR THE ENGAGEMENT, THE BATTLE OF THE LYS.

Left: *The Battle of the Lys. A British sentry beside a foot bridge over the Lys Canal at Saint-Floris. Petrol tins are on hand for burning the bridge should it be reported that the Germans are advancing nearby, 18 May 1918. (The Germans did not reach Saint-Floris.)*

Above: *The Battle of the Lys. German prisoners being guarded by Australians at Caëstre, 23 April 1918.*

The Germans called it Operation Georgette, a scaled-down version of a more ambitious plan: Operation George. The German Sixth Army's objective was the key Allied rail centre at Hazebrouck. From here the whole area north and west to the Channel was occupied by a mass of British logistic installations and reinforcement depots. German tactics were a repeat of Operation Michael: a massive artillery bombardment, followed by storm troop penetration, aided by thick fog. On this occasion there was an additional factor in their favour: part of the sector astride Neuve Chapelle was held by a poorly-equipped, badly-led Portuguese division with low morale. They broke almost immediately. The 50th and 51st Divisions were used to plug the gap in the line left by the Portuguese, arriving to find it held by the

Below: The Battle of the Lys (Operation Georgette). A Machine Gun Corps post in a barn near Haverskerque, 1 May 1918.

11th Cyclist Battalion and King Edward's Horse. The 1st Australian Division, having just reached Amiens from Messines, was ordered north to cover Hazebrouck, and arrived on 12 April to relieve British troops, including the 4th Guards Brigade, which was putting up an epic defence. The Germans were eventually held five miles from Hazebrouck.

On 10 April, the German Fourth Army attacked the Messines ridge and seized Mount Kemmel. The battle had now become the Fourth Battle of Ypres, with General Sir Herbert Plumer in charge of the British side, as he had been for the Third Battle (which is often known, after just one of its phases, as "Passchendaele"). It was a time of great trial for the British. Ferdinand Foch, the Allied Commander-in-Chief, initially refused to relieve British divisions in the middle of the battle, convinced that Georgette was a diversion from a major attack in Picardy. On 11 April, Haig, not a man given to making proclamations, issued an order of the day:

THE LYS OFFENSIVE, APRIL 1918

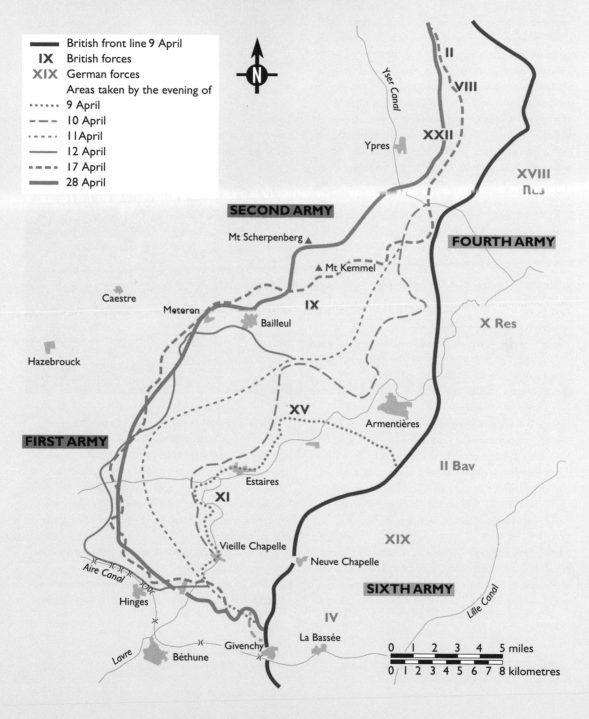

Legend:
- British front line 9 April
- **IX** British forces
- **XIX** German forces
- Areas taken by the evening of
- 9 April
- 10 April
- 11 April
- 12 April
- 17 April
- 28 April

N

SECOND ARMY

Mt Scherpenberg ▲

▲ Mt Kemmel

Caestre

Meteren

Bailleul

Hazebrouck

IX

FOURTH ARMY

Yser Canal

Ypres

II

VIII

XXII

XVIII Res

X Res

XV

Armentières

II Bav

FIRST ARMY

Estaires

XI

Vieille Chapelle

XIX

Neuve Chapelle

SIXTH ARMY

Aire Canal

Hinges

IV

La Bassée

Lille Canal

Lavre

Béthune

Givenchy

| 0 | 1 | 2 | 3 | 4 | 5 miles |
| 0 | 1 | 2 3 4 5 6 7 | 8 kilometres |

GEORGES CLEMENCEAU

Nicknamed "the Tiger", Clemenceau was a combative character throughout his life. While at medical school he demonstrated against the Second Empire of Napoleon III and spent a short time in prison. As Mayor of Montmartre during the Franco-Prussian war, he helped organize the Republican Guard to defend Paris. As a journalist he passionately defended the wrongly convicted Captain Alfred Dreyfus. He held political office as Interior Minister and Prime Minister from 1906 to 1909. In the lead-up to the First World War he campaigned for France to increase the size of the army and stand up to Germany. His inaugural address to the National Assembly on becoming Prime Minister on 20 November 1917 included the phrase: "War. Nothing but war". He was a scathing critic of the French failure to wage war successfully, and set about restoring national morale. He was responsible for selecting Foch as the overall Allied commander, over the head of Pétain, whom he judged as too defensively minded. Clemenceau suppressed pacifist pamphlets, arrested several prominent defeatists, and put others on trial for treason. His actions played a major part in restoring French morale for the final year of the war. He well deserved the other nickname he acquired – *Père la victoire* (Father Victory).

There is no course open to us but to fight it out! Every position must be held to the last man: there must be no retirement. With our backs to the wall and believing in the justice of our cause, each one of us must fight on to the end. The safety of our homes and the freedom of mankind alike depend on the conduct of each of us at this critical moment.

While Haig's soldiers were fighting to stave off disaster, British Prime Minister Lloyd George had been attacked in the House of Commons for denying Haig the reinforcements he had repeatedly asked for. By "creative accounting", Lloyd George persuaded members that the BEF was actually stronger than in the previous year by some 218,000 men, failing to mention that this figure included 335,454 men in the Labour Corps. Furthermore, the percentage of infantrymen in the army had shrunk drastically, and the infantry divisions were the key formations needed for the type of fighting the BEF was experiencing.

Meanwhile on 17/18 April, while the BEF's attention was concentrated in Flanders, the German effort to take Amiens, in Picardy, south of the Georgette sector, was renewed. On 24 April, an attack with tanks broke

Top right: The Battle of the Lys. Outpost manned by men of the 11th Battalion, Argyll and Sutherland Highlanders on a road beside the Lys Canal near Saint-Floris, 9 May 1918.

Bottom right: British soldiers holding a street barricade in Bailleul just before the fall of the town 15 April 1918.

through to take Villers-Bretonneux. A counter-attack consisting of a pincer movement by two Australian brigades, the 13th and 15th, succeeded in retaking the town. The Australians had once again set the Germans back in their attempts to advance on this key communications centre.

Back in Flanders, Mount Kemmel (now held by the French) was taken by the German Alpine Corps on 25 April; but by failing to take Cassel and Mont des Cats as well, the Germans were denied the chance of cutting the line of communication to Ypres. Doing so would have forced the BEF to evacuate the Ypres Salient and the Yser position. In the event no great strategic gain was made; the Channel ports were not taken. The second great offensive had not achieved its aim.

Many of the British soldiers in this battle were young conscripts, barely eighteen and a half years old, and with hardly sufficient training. But, although their performance was patchy at times, they held. An officer of the Alpine Corps with much battle experience told a British officer after the war: "I think I may say that the defenders on the British front in April 1918 were the best troops of the many with whom we crossed swords in the course of the four and a quarter years." A German assessment concluded that their own armies on the Flanders front "had exhausted their powers of attack".

On 29 April, Georgette, or the Battle of the Lys, ended. The cost was less than half of the shorter Michael offensive in Picardy, but heavy enough: Allied casualties numbered 111,300. The combined cost of Michael and Georgette was 351,793 Allied casualties (dead, wounded, missing and prisoners) and 348,300 German – a total of over 700,000 casualties in less than a month and a half.

Top left: *A German soldier sits on a corduroy road in the marshlands near Armentières, next to signs in English and German, 1918.*

Bottom left: *German troops in Armentières, 1918.*

THE GERMAN MAY/JUNE OFFENSIVES

ERICH VON LUDENDORFF'S OFFENSIVES WERE AIMED AT WINNING THE WAR BEFORE THE AMERICANS DEPLOYED IN STRENGTH. AT FIRST GLANCE, IT SEEMED THAT HE MIGHT SUCCEED.

Although by 1 May there were over 200,000 US troops in France (140,000 infantry), these represented only nine undertrained divisions, of which two were incomplete (an American division at 26,000 men was twice the size of a French or British one). Furthermore, the French and British provided the artillery and transport in all American divisions. The American Expeditionary Force (AEF) commander, General John Pershing, had specific instructions from the US government not to commit his formations piecemeal, but only as one national army. But he realized that he might be forced to deploy parts of his army if his allies

Left: *The Third Battle of the Aisne. German 10-cm, long-barrelled guns firing a barrage in support of stormtroopers in the Montdidier-Noyon sector, June 1918.*

Above: *The Third Battle of the Aisne. German infantry reserves advancing towards the front line during the assault on the Chemin des Dames.*

risked being defeated. Meanwhile, all was not well with Germany, whose armies had suffered massive casualties, and there were worrying signs that morale and discipline in some formations were deteriorating – mainly for lack of experienced, well-trained officers.

Ludendorff was convinced that Flanders was the best place to attack, offering the prospect of driving the British back to the sea. However, Foch had sent 17 French divisions to this sector in response to Haig's request for assistance during the March and April battles. In order to pull the French south before attacking in Flanders, the Germans directed their next offensive in Champagne and on the Chemin des Dames Ridge.

Ludendorff's third offensive started on 27 May with an attack by 17 German divisions, supported by 4,000 guns and numerous mortars. The Allies, including all the senior French commanders, were taken by surprise. Part of the attack hit four exhausted British divisions sent to recuperate in this "quiet sector". The Germans broke through on a 25-mile front. By 3 June, in a repeat of August 1914, the Germans stood on the River Marne near Château-Thierry, a mere 56 miles from Paris.

GENERAL JOHN PERSHING COMMANDING AMERICAN EXPEDITIONARY FORCE

Pershing first saw active service in the last of the frontier campaigns in the American West in 1891. He served in the Spanish–American War in Cuba where one officer described him as "cool as a bowl of cracked ice" under fire. Sent to the Philippines in 1899, he led expeditions against the Moros, and later became governor of the Moro province, successfully stamping out the insurrection there. As a Major General in 1916/17, he commanded the force chasing the bandit Pancho Villa in Mexico. When America entered the First World War in April 1917, Pershing was appointed over the heads of several more senior officers to command the AEF, and in May 1917 arrived in France with his staff, but without an army. The build-up of American troops from a tiny regular army was painfully slow, but only to be expected: there was so much that had to be done to prepare them for battle. For the next year as American troops began to arrive in France, Pershing resisted Allied demands to amalgamate his troops with existing British and French formations, instead forming US divisions, corps and armies. Although the Allies, short of men, argued for amalgamation, Pershing steadfastly refused, for perfectly understandable reasons of national pride. This was a risky decision, because the Germans might succeed in inflicting such a severe defeat on the French and British that the war would be over before

the Americans could take part. Although one could argue that when and where to commit American troops was a decision the US government should have made, the responsibility passed to Pershing. It is to his credit that he withstood exhortations from Allied politicians and generals to change his mind, many of the latter of whom had vastly more experience in major war than he.

THE AISNE,
MAY–JUNE 1918

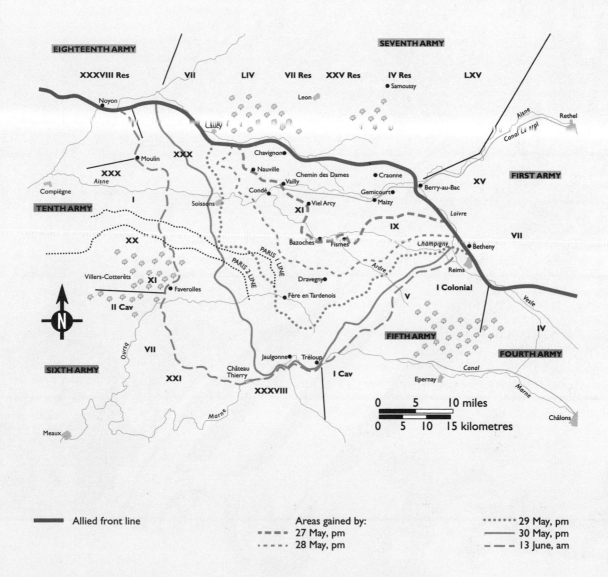

EIGHTEENTH ARMY

XXXVIII Res   VII   LIV   VII Res   XXV Res   IV Res   LXV

SEVENTH ARMY

Noyon

Samoussy

Leon

Aisne

Rethel

Canal Lateral

Lauey

Chavignon

XXX

Moulin

XXX

Aisne

Compiègne

TENTH ARMY

I

Nauville

Chemin des Dames

Vailly

Condé

Craonne

Berry-au-Bac

XV

FIRST ARMY

Soissons

XI

Viel Arcy

Gemicourt

Maizy

Loivre

IX

VII

XX

Bazoches

Fismes

Champigny

Betheny

PARIS LINE

PARIS 2 LINE

Villers-Cotterêts

XI

Faverolles

Dravegny

Fère en Tardenois

Ardre

Reims

Vesle

V

I Colonial

IV

II Cav

Oursq

VII

FIFTH ARMY

FOURTH ARMY

Epernay

Canal

SIXTH ARMY

XXI

Château
Thierry

Jaulgonne

Tréloup

I Cav

Marne

Châlons

Marne

XXXVIII

Meaux

0	5	10 miles
0	5	10 15 kilometres

N

Allied front line

Areas gained by:
- – – – 27 May, pm
- – – – 28 May, pm
- · · · · 29 May, pm
- ——— 30 May, pm
- – – – 13 June, am

This page: *German troops at Mount Kemmel, May 1918.*

Top: *The Third Battle of the Aisne. German infantry working forward through the village of Pont-Arcy, taken from the British IX Corps on 27 May 1918.*

Bottom: *The Third Battle of the Aisne (Blücher-Yorck Offensive). German troops working forward in groups across the Aisne canal, during the attack upon Fismes, 27 May 1918.*

ATTACK ON FRENCH LINES,
9 JUNE 1918

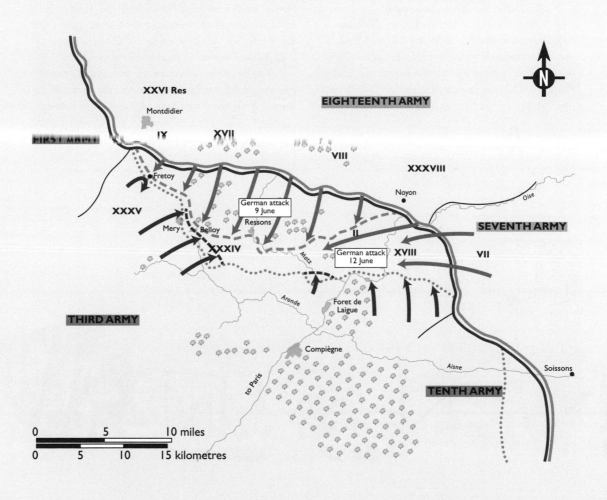

XXVI Res

Montdidier

EIGHTEENTH ARMY

FIRST ARMY

IX

XVII

VIII

XXXVIII

Fretoy

Noyon

Oise

XXXV

German attack
9 June

Ressons

II

SEVENTH ARMY

Mery

Belloy

XXXIV

German attack
12 June

XVIII

VII

Matz

Aronde

Foret de
Laigue

THIRD ARMY

Compiègne

Aisne

Soissons

to Paris

TENTH ARMY

0   5   10 miles

0   5   10   15 kilometres

——— French front line, 9 June

——▶ French counter attack, 11 June onwards

▪▪▪▪ French positions, 11 June

——— German front line, 9 June

– – – German advance, 9 June

▪▪▪▪ German furthest advance

The British suffered 28,703 casualties (dead, wounded, missing and prisoners); French losses totalled 96,160. The reputations of French commanders, including that of Foch, were diminished. Paradoxically, Haig's standing improved, rallying after political confidence in him dipped, caused by the reverses of March and April. Foch began to consult him and heed his recommendations more readily.

On 1 June, the US 2nd and 3rd Infantry Divisions moved up to defend Château-Thierry, and on 6 June attacked at Belleau Wood, a strongly held square mile of woods and rocks about ten miles north-west of Chateau-Thierry. This was not the first American attack of the war – that occurred in the Somme, when the 28th Regiment of

the US 1st Division captured the village of Cantigny on 28 May. This engagement took place over a year after America had entered the war, an indication of just how unprepared the US was.

On 9 June, Ludendorff's fourth attack, by the Eighteenth and Seventh Armies between Montdidier and Noyon, made some gains. But a Franco-American counter-attack halted the Eighteenth Army by 11 June. By the next day, the Seventh Army's offensive had also been stopped.

Ludendorff decided to make one last attack before switching his efforts to Flanders. He intended to surround the strongly defended city of Reims by a pincer attack: the Seventh Army attacking on the western side and turning

Below: *The Third Battle of the Aisne. German infantry advancing over a captured trench during the attack between Montdidier and Noyon, June 1918.*

east up the Marne, while the First Army headed south for Châlons-sur-Marne. Forewarned by deserters and air reconnaissance, the French Fourth Army stopped the German First Army in its tracks. The German Seventh Army, up against lighter opposition, reached the Marne, and about 11 divisions managed to cross. But the advance was held by the US 3rd Division, whose stubborn defence, especially that of the 38th Infantry Regiment, earned it the title "the Rock of the Marne". The whole attack was blocked when Allied aircraft and artillery destroyed all the German bridges, cutting their lines of communication.

Ludendorff, realizing that he had failed, and now desperately short of men and needing to shorten the line, pulled back from the Soissons–Château-Thierry–Reims salient. Since 21 March, the German Army had suffered around half a million casualties. Allied losses were around the same, but American troops were pouring in at a rate of some 300,000 a month. On the other hand, Ludendorff had used up all the men released from the east by the surrender of Russia. Ludendorff had "talked up" his offensives as being the harbingers of victory that would usher in peace. When his promises failed to materialize, morale in the German Army and among the civilian population plummeted. From this point, strategic initiative passed to the Allies.

PART 2
WAR IN THE AIR AND AT SEA

CHARLES J. DE LACY.
1918.

ZEEBRUGGE,
23 APRIL 1918

IN THE FIRST WORLD WAR, AS IN THE SECOND, THE GREATEST THREAT TO THE UNITED KINGDOM'S SURVIVAL WAS THE U-BOAT. AT ONE POINT IN 1917, IT SEEMED THAT THE UK WOULD BE STARVED INTO SUBMISSION. BY 1918, THE THREAT HAD RECEDED, THANKS TO THE INTRODUCTION OF CONVOYS.

But submarines and coastal forces operating from Bruges remained a threat to shipping supplying the armies in France and Allied vessels in the North Sea. The German naval base at Bruges, eight miles inland, was connected to Zeebrugge and Ostend by canals, whose locks allowed vessels to come and go at any state of the tide. The reinforced concrete shelters housing about 18 submarines and up to 25 destroyers

VICE-ADMIRAL ROGER KEYES

Keyes joined the Royal Navy as a cadet in 1885, serving as a junior officer on anti-slavery patrols in the Indian Ocean and during the Boxer Rebellion in China. At the outbreak of the First World War, he commanded the 8th Submarine Flotilla based at Harwich, taking part in the Battle of Heligoland Bight, commanding his submarines from the destroyer *Lurcher*. He was heavily involved in the Dardanelles campaign as chief of staff to Vice-Admiral Sackville Carden, then to Vice-Admiral John de Robeck. He personally led some of the attempts to clear the mines, commanding from the cruiser *Amethyst*, which was badly damaged by Turkish guns. On promotion to Rear Admiral he took command of the 4th Battle Squadron in the Grand Fleet in June 1916. After a spell as Director of Plans in the Admiralty, he was appointed Flag Officer of the Dover Patrol. His tactics produced a higher success rate in sinking U-boats than his predecessor. He planned and personally led the raids on Ostend and Zeebrugge.

Left: One of HMS Vindictive's *funnels shredded by shrapnel in the Zeebrugge Raid.*

Previous page: A painting by Charles de Lacy of HMS Vindictive *alongside the Mole at Zeebrugge, as the storming parties climb the brows onto the Mole. The* Daffodil *is keeping* Vindictive *in position.*

Above: *The cruiser HMS* Vindictive, *showing upper deck with wooden brows rigged for landing parties, before the raid on Zeebrugge, which took place on 23 April 1918.*

were immune to the bombs of that period. Vice Admiral Keyes, commanding the Dover Patrol, accordingly developed a plan to block the canal exits at Zeebrugge and Ostend.

The 4th Battalion Royal Marines (4 RM) formed the main storming force for the Zeebrugge operation, backed up by a seaman party 150 strong, and a demolition party of 72 Royal Marines and seamen. The battalion comprised both Royal Marine Artillery (RMA) and Royal Marines Light Infantry (RMLI). The RMA manned howitzers, pom-poms, Lewis guns and mortars on the decks of HMS *Vindictive* to provide supporting

fire during the assault by the RMLI on the Mole at Zeebrugge. During the training period for the operation, the battalion was told that any man who did not wish to go could pull out (the mission was not specified). No one did, so in effect the whole battalion were volunteers.

The storming parties were embarked in the old cruiser HMS *Vindictive* and two Mersey river ferries, the *Iris* and *Daffodil*. On *Vindictive*'s port side, 14 narrow wooden brows, or gangplanks, had been fitted, to enable the storming parties to run from the ship onto the Mole. *Vindictive* was to secure alongside the Mole using specially designed grapnels. *Iris* likewise,

THE ZEEBRUGGE MOLE MISSION

This is the plan of Zeebrugge Mole prepared by Vice-Admiral Keyes for the attack on 22/23 April 1918, and was included in his report. The principal objective of the storming party was the capture of the 4.1-inch battery (see arrow). The Royal Marines were to secure Number Three Shed to prevent attack up the Mole, then advance as far as the seaplane base. The demolition party was to "inflict as much damage as was possible" on the harbour works and defences. The canal entrance was to be closed by three blockships: *Thetis* would ram the lock gates, and *Intrepid* and *Iphigenia* would be run ashore at the southern end of the escalade. Two submarines loaded with explosive were to ram the viaduct connecting the Mole to the shore, and crews were to set fuses to blow up the boats, after having left by small boat first.

On the seaward side the Mole rose about 30 feet above the sea at high water. On the top there was a raised pathway about 10 feet wide, with a drop of about 16 feet from the raised pathway to the Mole itself.

The sketch below right shows the intended and actual position of *Vindictive*, the actual positions of attacking ships while landing parties were on the Mole, the barge and net booms that caused the *Thetis* to ground early, and the final positions of the blockships.

After the raid, the Germans managed to dredge a canal round the blockships. Because Ostend was not blocked, submarines and destroyers could still access Bruges.

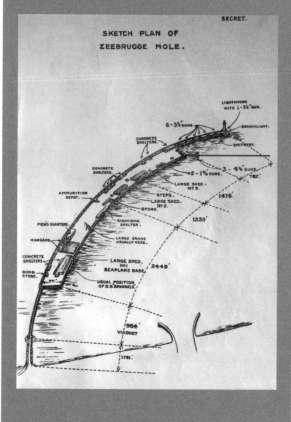

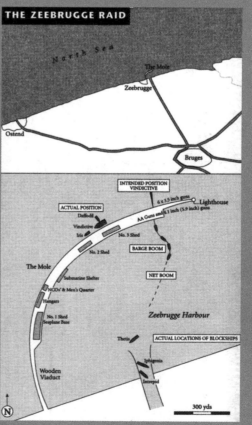

just ahead of *Vindictive*, while *Daffodil* pushed against *Vindictive*'s starboard side to keep her hard against the Mole. In essence the job of 4 RM and the other storming parties was to destroy as many as possible of the guns on the Mole – to prevent, or at least distract, them from engaging the block ships as they approached. There was no storming party for the Ostend operation.

Below: *Kaiser Wilhelm II viewing the damage done to the Mole by the blowing-up of Submarine C3. This photograph was taken only a few hours after the successful attack on the Mole at Zeebrugge, St George's Day, 1918.*

After midnight on 23 April, *Vindictive* approached the Mole at Zeebrugge, illuminated by searchlights from the shore, her upperworks swept by fire causing heavy casualties among the troops waiting to climb the brows. Captain Carpenter, commanding *Vindictive*, had increased speed to close the Mole, but in doing so put her alongside 300 yards further south than intended. Consequently, landing parties were much further from their objectives; *Vindictive*'s guns could not be brought to bear in their support, and German batteries on the northern end of the Mole were left free to flay *Vindictive* at point-blank range. Of 14 brows, only two could be dropped initially, followed by another two. The special

MAJOR EDWARD BAMFORD VC DSO RMLI, OC B COMPANY 4TH BATTALION ROYAL MARINES

This portrait was painted after the War, when Bamford was serving in a ship on the China Station. Of the seven Victoria Crosses (VCs) awarded to the Royal Navy and Royal Marines for the action at Zeebrugge, four were elected by ballot under Rule 13 of the Royal Warrant, which allowed for a VC to be awarded on the result of a ballot by the man's peers. Captain, as he was then, Bamford was one such recipient. As HMS *Vindictive* was approaching the Mole, both the commanding officer and second-in-command of 4 RM were killed. The Adjutant, Captain Arthur Chater, took command. And at a crucial stage in the battle with the plan unravelling, he restored momentum with Captain Bamford whose, in Chater's words, "totally unperturbed manner had the most reassuring effect on all who came in contact with him that night".

On return to Deal after the operation, the survivors of the battalion were balloted. Bamford and Sergeant Norman Finch were selected by their comrades to be awarded the VC.

grapnels proved useless, and the *Daffodil*, having shoved *Vindictive* against the wall as planned, had to keep her pinned there for the whole 55 minutes the landing parties were ashore. The heavily laden assault parties – having lurched up the steeply inclined see-sawing ladders as *Vindictive* rolled in the swell shuddering with the explosions of shells on her upperworks – jumped down to find the plan was unravelling. Only a quarter of many of these parties made it up the brow. The *Iris* never managed to land the Royal Marines of A Company 4 RM she carried. When her captain Commander Valentine Gibbs laid her alongside the Mole, the grapnels would not hold her. All efforts to secure her were in vain and all the time she was under heavy fire. One shell hit a group of 56 men, killing 49 and wounding the remainder. Gibbs was mortally wounded with both legs blown off. Another shell killed or wounded all the A Company officers.

When the withdrawal was signalled, few of the objectives had been gained, except that the submarine

C3 crammed with charges was run in under the wooden viaduct. Her crew lit the fuses and escaped in a small boat. The explosion cut the Mole off from the shore. Although the members of the landing parties came away thinking they had failed, air reconnaissance in the morning showed that the canal entrance was blocked. The raid on Ostend failed, as did a subsequent attempt there.

The total British casualties at Zeebrugge were 170 dead, 400 wounded and 45 missing (of 730 all ranks in 4 RM, there were 360 casualties, including 17 officers of whom 10 were killed). But morale soared in Britain after Zeebrugge. The years of waiting, seemingly only reacting to German sorties, and the dreadful losses exacted by U-boats had sapped the public's faith in the Royal Navy. The German March offensive in France had dealt a blow to their confidence in the outcome of the war. The Zeebrugge raid provided a ray of hope among the gloom.

This *page: HMS* Vindictive *on return from the Zeebrugge raid with extensive damage.*

THE WAR
AT SEA

ALTHOUGH THE INTRODUCTION OF THE CONVOY SYSTEM IN APRIL 1917 HAD REVERSED THE RATE OF MERCHANT SHIP LOSSES TO U-BOATS, WHICH HAD THREATENED TO BRING BRITAIN TO HER KNEES, THEY STILL REMAINED A POTENT MENACE.

Throughout the First World War a major problem was detecting a U-boat when it had dived. This was only made possible by sonar (sound navigation and ranging), which did not enter service with the Royal Navy until just before the outbreak of the Second World War. Hydrophones could sometimes detect a dived submarine, but a ship dipping hydrophones into the sea to listen for a submarine had to stop; the sound of its own wash and propeller blanked out the noise of the submarine. Remaining stationary when submarines were about was an invitation to be torpedoed, so it was not recommended. Hydrophones were credited with locating, and subsequently destroying, just three U-boats in four and a half years of war. At night, U-boats often attacked

Left: *Two British submarines alongside a depot ship.*

Above: *HMS* Furious *after conversion in early 1918, but still with central bridge and funnel, which caused too much turbulence over the landing deck aft to recover aircraft. Aircraft could still be launched from the flying-off deck forward. She launched a successful raid on the Zeppelin sheds at Tønder in Schleswig-Holstein on 19 July 1918.* Furious *was later converted to a proper flush-deck carrier, and served in the Second World War.*

Above: *Felixstowe F.2A flying boat in flight during an anti-submarine patrol. The dazzle camouflage schemes adopted by these aircraft aided identification in the air during combat and on the water in the event of being forced down.*

on the surface, their low silhouette making them difficult to spot. Convoy escorts lacked radar, which had yet to be invented, so U-boats were able to slip past convoy escorts at night, and able to shadow convoys even in daylight in poor visibility.

British submarines accounted for some 18 U-boats. This involved catching the enemy on the surface. The technology of the time did not allow a submerged boat to "kill" another submerged boat. The danger in using submarines to hunt U-boats was that all ships and aircraft were prone to regard any submerged craft as hostile and attack on sight. Consequently there were several British submarines lost in "blue on blue" encounters. .

The war against the U-boat was just as fiercely

contested in the Mediterranean as in the Atlantic. Indeed one successful U-boat ace, Karl Dönitz (Commander-in-Chief U-boats in the Second World War), operated exclusively in the Mediterranean. He was convinced that the convoy was the key to the Allied defeat of the U-boat. But success seldom came easily, as the experience of the sloop HMS *Hollyhock*, escorting a convoy in March 1918 in the Mediterranean, showed. The engagement started just after lunch, when a U-boat torpedoed a ship, without sinking it. About an hour later another U-boat attacked the other side of the convoy, but was seen off when HMS *Campanula* depth-charged it. At teatime, a torpedo track running parallel with the convoy was spotted by *Hollyhock*. Another escort, the

Above: Furious *with Camels ranged on her foredeck.*

CONVOYS

The British Admiralty resisted introducing the convoy system until 1917 for a number of reasons, including:

- The misapprehension that Merchant Navy skippers would not be able to steam in convoy formation, despite the fact that troopships had crossed the channel in convoys since 1914, without one vessel being lost. Other cross-channel and North Sea traffic had been convoyed with very few losses.
- The misconception that escorts would be better employed "hunting" U-boats because protecting

convoys was too passive. But convoying actually presented the opportunity to act offensively against U-boats attacking the convoy. Although this was a bonus, because the safe arrival of the merchant ships and their cargoes, not sinking enemy submarines was what counted and was the aim of the game. Using escorts and aircraft to hunt U-boats in waters where there was no convoy was a waste of time and precious resources – the presence of a U-boat in such areas was irrelevant; there was nothing there except fish.

Morvada, engaged with her 4.7-inch gun and dropped depth charges. A torpedo was spotted, and was engaged with gunfire. Eventually the warhead was knocked off by gunfire, but did not explode. Next morning a submarine was sighted on the convoy's port side, and engaged by two escorts who sank the boat. At noon the convoy was attacked again, fire was returned but with no damage to either side. At 5.00 pm another attack was made. One of *Hollyhock*'s officers wrote later, "But we managed to thwart Fritz … Truly this region off Cape Bon is a very hot place, submarines seem to swarm there.

Left: A North Sea airship of the Royal Naval Air Service.

They were sighted in 24 different places in this area during two days."

The Royal Naval Air Service (RNAS) had a leading role neutralizing the German light cruiser *Breslau* and battle cruiser *Goeben*. In the first days of the war they had sailed from the Adriatic to Constantinople to join with the Turkish navy, making fools of the Royal Navy. In January 1918, they left the Dardanelles for the Aegean. Spotted by the RNAS, they were harried with bombs and by destroyers vectored by the RNAS. *Breslau* eventually struck a mine and sank, while *Goeben* limped ignominiously back to Constantinople.

The RNAS were key players in anti-submarine operations in the Mediterranean and the North Sea.

COMMODORE REGINALD TYRWHITT

Tyrwhitt, an aggressive and skilled fighting sailor, commanded the Harwich Force with distinction throughout the First World War. He joined the Royal Navy as a cadet in 1883. Before 1914 he commanded six ships, and three destroyer flotillas. At the Battle of Heligoland, he led a force of two cruisers and 31 destroyers. He was in action on numerous occasions throughout the war, including the Cuxhaven Raid, the Battle of Dogger Bank, and the Zeebrugge and Ostend Raids. On 11 August 1918 during an action at Terschelling, off the Dutch coast, involving German aircraft and British motor boats, the Harwich Force lured a Zeppelin L-35 further out to sea, where it was shot down by Lieutenant Stuart Culley in a Sopwith Camel, which had been launched from a lighter towed by the destroyer *Redoubt*. Tyrwhitt signalled to his Force, Hymn 227, A&M, v.7:

Oh Happy Band of Pilgrims,
Look upward to the skies
Where such a light affliction
Shall win so great a prize.

Tyrwhitt was promoted to Rear Admiral and created a baronet of Terschelling and Oxford in December 1919.

Airships and flying boats could spot U-boat periscopes and drop bombs, as well as alerting the escorts. Their presence over a convoy could act as a "scarecrow", keeping the boat dived and discouraging it from putting up its periscope and therefore "blind" and unable to track the convoy. A dived submarine could seldom keep up with a convoy.

Zeppelins were another threat, with long endurance and the ability to climb more swiftly than flying boats; they passed the position of convoys back to base by wireless (radio). Enemy destroyers, coastal forces and aircraft summoned by the Zeppelin would attack the convoy and its attendant airships and flying boats. To counter these, the RNAS devised a means of launching a Sopwith Camel from a lighter towed by a destroyer. On 11 August 1918 Lieutenant Culley in a Sopwith Camel, launched in this way, shot down a Zeppelin after which he landed in the sea and was picked up by a destroyer. A better solution to the Zeppelin, and to other schemes for using aircraft in a maritime role, would have been a fully flush-decked aircraft carrier. HMS *Furious* was not fully flush-decked. HMS *Argus* was the first full flush-deck British aircraft carrier, and the first in the world. She was converted from an ocean liner. She carried out trials in October 1918, but never took part in an operation. Two more were being built, but were not completed until after the war ended.

Below: *Lieutenant Stuart Douglas Culley RNAS flying a Sopwith Camel during a second and successful attempt to take off from a lighter being towed behind a Destroyer at 36 knots. This Sopwith Camel is on display in the First World War Galleries in the Imperial War Museum.*

THE WAR IN THE AIR

THE ROLE OF THE ROYAL FLYING CORPS (RFC) AT THE OUTBREAK OF WAR IN 1914 WAS SEEN AS PURELY RECONNAISSANCE – UNLIKE THE ROYAL NAVAL AIR SERVICE (RNAS), WHICH HAD FORESEEN AND PRACTISED A WIDER RANGE OF SKILLS, INCLUDING OFFENSIVE ACTION.

The RFC soon learned that the enemy would not allow them to reconnoitre unhindered, any more than they would allow the enemy similar freedom. The same applied to aircraft or balloons spotting for artillery. Information, whether obtained by eyeball or air photography, was something you had to fight for; hence the need for fighter aircraft to shoot down those snooping on you, and to protect your own snoopers. Throughout the war, reconnaissance and artillery co-operation remained the key activities of the aviators on both sides. But the publicity and glamour was reserved for the fighter pilots, especially the aces. Three of the most outstanding of these met their ends in 1918.

The most famous of German aces, leader of the "Flying Circus" with a score of 80 victories, Manfred von Richthofen, was shot down on 21 April 1918 through lack of judgement or carelessness. In retrospect he was probably suffering from combat fatigue, one of its symptoms being carelessness. The British ace, Edward "Mick" Mannock, whose comment on hearing of Richthofen's demise was "I hope he roasted all the way down", also died because he broke his own rules. Mannock, with 73 victories, was the most professional of aces. He should have been rested, but instead took over the Canadian ace William Bishop's Number 85 Squadron. But Mannock, like Richthofen, was very possibly careless, again with combat fatigue.

Left: *The cockpit of the SE5A, the type flown by James McCudden in 56 Squadron RFC, showing the machine gun and telescopic sight.*

Above: *Edward Mannock.*

Below: *A Fokker DR-1.*

MAJOR JAMES McCUDDEN

Shown here as an air mechanic, McCudden transferred from the Royal Engineers to the Royal Flying Corps in April 1913. The outbreak of war found him as an air mechanic in Number 3 Squadron RFC. He occasionally flew as a gunner in Morane aircraft, with his brother, a pilot, if he could. Though recommended for pilot training, McCudden was kept in France because of a shortage of mechanics. To mollify him he was allowed to fly as an observer. Eventually he was released to undergo pilot training, and by the spring of 1918 had risen through the ranks to become the leading "ace" of the RFC, flying SE5As in Number 56 Squadron RFC. In March 1918, he was ordered home for a rest. He regretted leaving flying and fighting, and admitted to weeping at the prospect – perhaps an indication that he needed a rest. It was to last four months. Posted as commanding officer of Number 56 Squadron, he was killed while flying to join his command when his engine failed on take-off.

Bishop, with 72 victories, who was rested, survived. The leading RFC ace James McCudden, joined the Royal Engineers in 1910 as a boy bugler. He was killed in an accident on take-off aged 23, decorated with the VC, DSO and bar, MC and bar, and MM.

Mannock's reference to "roasting" alludes to the fact that as neither side issued parachutes to their aircrew, many were burnt to death. The combination of petrol, and canvas and wood fuselages and wings, painted with highly inflammable waterproofing, or "dope", resulted in many aircraft catching fire when hit. Being quite light, they could take a long time to flutter down. Some aircrew jumped out to their deaths rather than face prolonged agony.

MANFRED ALBRECHT FREIHERR VON RICHTHOFEN, THE "RED BARON"

Richthofen, probably the most famous of all First World War aces, was originally a Prussian cavalry officer. He transferred to the German Army Air Service in May 1915. He flew as an observer on both the Eastern and Western Fronts, before becoming a pilot in reconnaissance aircraft at Verdun in early 1916. In August 1916 he joined Oswald Boelcke's Jagdstaffel 2 (Fighter Squadron) as a fighter pilot. In January 1917, Richthofen took command and by the end of April had scored 52 victories. In June he took command of Jagdgeschwader 1 (JG1), a fighter wing of four squadrons – the first of its type. JG1 became known as "Richthofen's Flying Circus" because its ground crews and support were transferred from one area of the front to another, moving like a travelling circus by train, and often living in tents. Allied propaganda depicted Richthofen as a ruthless killer and he became a hate figure in France and Britain. His final score was 80, higher than any other pilot on either side. On 21 April 1918 he was shot down by ground fire while flying a Fokker DR-1 in a dogfight against Sopwith Camels.

On 1 April 1918 the RNAS and RFC amalgamated to form the Royal Air Force (RAF). This may have seemed logical at the time, but was, in the opinion of one writer on air power, "almost a mad step", made in a mood of panic caused by pin-prick raids on Britain by German bombers and Zeppelins, whose total efforts throughout the war caused fewer casualties than one would find on a typical "quiet day" on the Western Front. At this time the fledgling RAF had three main tasks: providing support for the war at sea (formerly the RNAS's role); support for the army in all theatres of war; and a new one, strategic bombing of Germany. In order to find aircraft for strategic bombing, air support for the war at sea against the U-boats was reduced – despite the fact that if the U-boats won, Britain would be out of the war. This was the first, but sadly not the last, time the RAF was to have a dire effect on maritime affairs. Fortunately, support for the BEF on the Western Front was not affected, because the German offensives, starting with Operation Michael on 21 March 1918, saw the widespread use of aircraft on both sides in support of ground troops. This activity combined with air-to-air combat, reconnaissance and artillery co-operation resulted in a high rate of casualties – at one stage some 30 per cent per day in British squadrons. It is perhaps significant that Richthofen, Mannock and McCudden were all killed during the hectic spring and summer of 1918.

Meanwhile, Major General Hugh Trenchard, having been transferred from commanding the RFC in France to Chief of the Air Staff of the fledgling RAF, resigned after clashing with Lord Rothermere, the first Secretary of State for Air. Rothermere described him as an intolerant know-all, a man of "dull, unimaginative mind". Lord Beaverbrook remarked years later, "If Trenchard was the father of the RAF, he was a father who tried to strangle the infant at birth though he got credit for the grown man." Trenchard now took command of the RAF's "Independent Force" of long-range bombers, whose mission was the strategic bombing of Germany. It was hoped that this bombing would so demoralize the German population and cut production of war fighting equipment that it would lead to Germany suing for peace. Postwar analysis showed that this bombing was ineffective. German industry and the population were being starved by the maritime blockade, not by bombing. Despite this, between the world wars the RAF believed,

Above: *Hugh Trenchard as a major general commanding the RFC in France.*

and expounded, that the role of their service was strategic bombing at the expense of support for the navy and the army. Consequently when Hitler invaded France and Flanders in May 1940, the RAF was unable to support the BEF as it had in 1918. Support for the navy was similarly deficient. It was to take about three years to put matters right. Strategic bombing in the Second World War did not, by itself, lead to the defeat of Germany, as promised by the "bomber barons" of the RAF and USAAF, most of them young aviators in the First World War.

What the experience of war in the air in the First World War should have taught was that air forces are a supporting arm, an adjunct to the maritime and land wars. Historically an air force has won only one war in history – that against Japan, with the dropping of two atomic bombs. Missiles now deliver nuclear weapons, not aircraft.

PART 3
OTHER FRONTS

THE BATTLE OF THE PIAVE, ITALY

BEFORE THE FIRST WORLD WAR, ITALY WAS A MEMBER OF THE TRIPLE ALLIANCE WITH GERMANY AND AUSTRIA-HUNGARY. HOWEVER, BEFORE COMMITTING HERSELF ON THE OUTBREAK OF WAR, ITALY NEGOTIATED BOTH WITH HER PUTATIVE ALLIES AND THE ENTENTE TO SEE WHICH SIDE WOULD OFFER THE BEST BARGAIN.

In the Secret Treaty of London in April 1915 – in return for the Entente offer of South Tyrol, Trieste, Gorizia, Istria and northern Dalmatia, all to be taken from the Austro-Hungarian Empire – Italy changed sides. In late May 1915, the badly trained, ill-led Italian Army set about attacking up some of the steepest mountains in Europe. The Austro-Hungarians held the high ground, and hence had the advantage. Avalanches were an added hazard, which the Austro-Hungarians deliberately triggered to kill thousands of Italians. The Italian Commander-in-Chief, General Luigi Cadorna, a general of limited ability, lost thousands of men in 11 fruitless offensives on the Isonzo between June 1915 and September 1917. On 24 October 1917 the Austro-Hungarians, now reinforced with six German divisions, attacked at Caporetto. The small amount of ground Cadorna had gained at a huge cost in casualties was lost at Caporetto (the 12th Battle of the Isonzo), followed by a headlong retreat. Thanks in part to 11 Anglo-French divisions, speedily moved from the Western Front, the Italians eventually stopped running, and reorganized on the line of the Piave river; a retreat of some 70 miles to within a few miles of Venice, Padua and Verona. Cadorna was replaced by Armando Diaz.

THE PIAVE OFFENSIVE

The Austro-Hungarian offensive on the Piave was intended as a follow-up to their success at Caporetto. The Austro-Hungarian Army had now lost the support of German formations, withdrawn for their offensives on the Western Front. Logistic support for the Austro-Hungarian Army on lines of communication, some of which ran over Alpine passes, was more difficult than for the Italians, blessed by better communications, including the lateral road and rail network linking Venice, Padua, Vicenza and Verona; and forward to the battle zone. The Italian Army had received large quantities of arms from Britain and France, and was well sited for defence.

On 15 June the Austro-Hungarians launched two simultaneous attacks: one by Army Group Boroević towards Padua, the other by Army Group Conrad towards Verona. Conrad von Hötzendorf's thrust towards Verona gained some ground but was eventually halted and pushed back.

Svetozar Boroević von Bojna managed to cross the lower Piave on a wide front, and secured a bridgehead about three miles deep. He was halted when the river, swollen by unexpectedly heavy rain, burst its banks making logistic support almost impossible. The Italians added to his problems by bombing his supply line.

Left: *An Italian field artillery piece being used as an anti-aircraft gun at Monte Nero above Caporetto.*

Previous page: *Italian Alpini troops climbing up to a pass carrying their skis.*

PIAVE OFFENSIVE

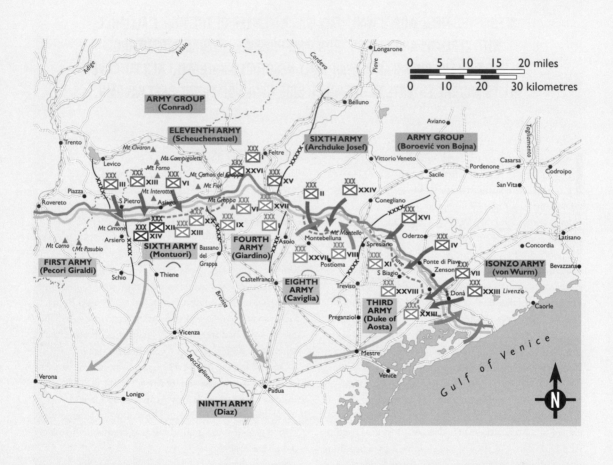

ARMY GROUP (Conrad)

ELEVENTH ARMY (Scheuchenstuel)

SIXTH ARMY (Archduke Josef)

ARMY GROUP (Boroević von Bojna)

FIRST ARMY (Pecori Giraldi)

SIXTH ARMY (Montuori)

FOURTH ARMY (Giardino)

EIGHTH ARMY (Caviglia)

THIRD ARMY (Duke of Aosta)

ISONZO ARMY (von Wurm)

NINTH ARMY (Diaz)

Gulf of Venice

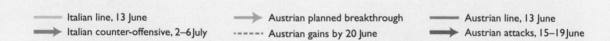

Italian line, 13 June   Austrian planned breakthrough   Austrian line, 13 June
Italian counter-offensive, 2–6 July   Austrian gains by 20 June   Austrian attacks, 15–19 June

Above: *Italian heavy artillery pieces being towed by tractors in the Piave river valley, Cadore region.*

FIELD MARSHAL COUNT FRANZ CONRAD VON HÖTZENDORF

Hötzendorf was chief of staff of the Austro-Hungarian Army at the outbreak of war, having held that post since 1906. In the pre-war period his aggressive demands for surprise attacks on Serbia and Italy led to his dismissal. Reinstated in December 1912, he was a key supporter of the hard line ultimatums to Serbia following the assassination of Crown Prince Franz Ferdinand at Sarajevo in June 1914. These were designed to be impossible to accept, so that the Austro-Hungarian Empire could invade and dispose of the hated Serbs forever. Thus Conrad von Hötzendorf can be said to be one of the handful of men who instigated the First World War, which ultimately destroyed the Habsburg Empire about which he cared so deeply. Having taken part in the Galician campaign, and initiated the Central Powers' invasion of Serbia, he clashed with the new emperor, Karl, and was dismissed on 1 March 1917. Given command of an army group for the Caporetto offensive, and after commanding one wing of the abortive Piave offensive, he was finally dismissed from command.

Above: *In the centre, Field Marshal Lord Horatio Kitchener (British Secretary of State for War), with General Armando Diaz on his right, and on his left General Luigi Cadorna (Chief of the Italian General Staff) at the Italian Headquarters.*

FIELD MARSHAL SVETOZAR BOROEVIĆ VON BOJNA

Boroević was a Croat infantry officer who was a corps commander in the Austro-Hungarian Army at the outbreak of the war. Promoted to army commander for the campaigns in Galicia, he was transferred to the Italian front to command the Fifth Army, which participated in all the 11 Battles of the Isonzo. Thanks in part to the participation of German formations, the Fifth Army won its greatest victory at Caporetto, for which Boroević was promoted to field marshal in January 1918. He opposed the Piave offensive, and his army group was defeated there. In the breakup of the Habsburg Empire in November 1918, he offered his services to the Croat representatives in Belgrade. This move was regarded as dangerously disloyal and he was forced to retire.

On the other hand, the Italians were able to use their lateral communications to bring up reinforcements from the Ninth Army, situated to the south of Padua. Pinned with his back to a flooded river, with most of his bridges washed away in the spate, and short of supplies, Boroević retreated on the night of 22/23 June.

The Austro-Hungarians lost around 70,000 men. The Italians suffered some 85,000 casualties. But the after-effects of the Austro-Hungarian defeat were profoundly felt in the ramshackle Habsburg Empire, with its multitude of diverse races, all with their own aspirations. It began to fall apart in all aspects — politically, militarily

and racially. For example, there were tales that Italian success on the Piave was partially due to Hungarian deserters betraying the plan to the Italians. General Ludendorff's caustic assessment of the Habsburg Empire, and how he assessed its value as an ally was, he said, "like being shackled to a corpse".

To Foch's irritation, General Diaz did not follow up the Austro-Hungarian withdrawal. This was probably a wise decision – he wanted to regroup and avoid premature attacks, which might undo the rise in morale that followed seeing off the enemy offensive. He would wait until autumn before attacking.

Below: *Italian lancers on the Piave front, 1918.*

Next page: *Captured Italian soldiers huddled in a trench on the Piave river front.*

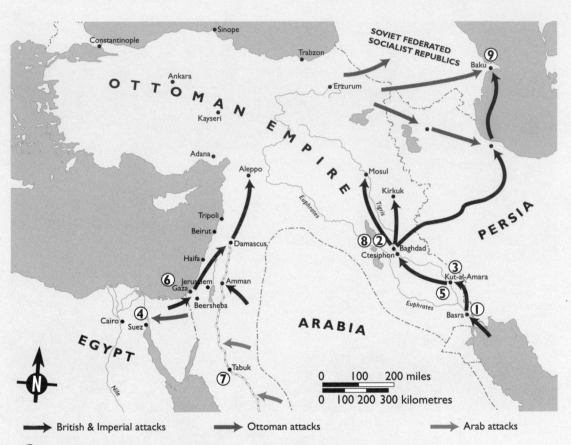

THE MIDDLE EAST
1914–1918

9

British & Imperial attacks ➤➤➤   Ottoman attacks ➤➤➤   Arab attacks ➤➤➤

① October 1914: Allied expedition sent to Mesopotamia to protect British oilfields. 6th Indian Division occupies Basra 14–23 November 1914

② Townshend advances towards Baghdad but is halted at Ctesiphon and driven back to Kut, 5 December 1915

③ Townshend's 13,500 troops are beseiged at Kut and finally surrender to the Ottomans on 29 April 1916

④ 1–3 February 1915: Ottoman forces attack Suez Canal

⑤ British and Imperial forces under General Frederick Maude retake Kut, February 1917

⑥ General Sir Archibald Murray advances across Sinai in 1915–16 and attacks Gaza in early 1917

⑦ 1917–18: Under the leadership of Thomas Edward Lawrence, Arab irregulars divert Ottoman troops from Palestine

⑧ Maude occupies Baghdad, 11 March 1917. Advance continues until Armistice with the Ottoman Empire signed, October 1918

⑨ British forces occupy Baku, September 1918, until expelled by the Ottoman forces

THE TURKISH FRONTS IN THE MIDDLE EAST

BY THE BEGINNING OF 1918, THE TWO CAMPAIGNS BEING FOUGHT BY THE BRITISH AGAINST TURKEY IN MESOPOTAMIA AND PALESTINE WERE WITHIN SIGHT OF BEING WON, ALTHOUGH THE FIGHTING LASTED UNTIL OCTOBER THAT YEAR. BOTH WERE ENTIRELY BRITISH "SHOWS" – TO USE THE EXPRESSION OF THE TIME. MESOPOTAMIA (IN BRITISH ARMY SLANG, "MESPOT") IS NOW IRAQ. THE PALESTINE CAMPAIGN WAS FOUGHT IN PARTS OF EGYPT (SINAI) IN PALESTINE AND WHAT IS NOW ISRAEL, AND PARTS OF WHAT ARE NOW SAUDI ARABIA, JORDAN, AND SYRIA.

MESOPOTAMIA

In October 1914, troops of the British Indian Army landed at Basra and seized the Anglo-Persian oil refinery at Abadan (British controlling shares were bought by Churchill as First Sea Lord just before the war to fuel the Royal Navy's super-dreadnought battleships – until now the Navy's capital ships had been coal-fired). The government of British India commanded and controlled the campaign, with a deal of interference from the War Council in London. The majority of troops involved throughout were from the Indian sub-continent. In essence the British planned a two-pronged advance along the Tigris and Euphrates rivers; the ultimate objective – Baghdad. All appeared to be going well until a force under Major-General Sir Charles Vere Ferrers Townshend, having overreached itself, surrendered to the Turks at Kut-al-Amara, on the Tigris, on 29 April 1916, after a four-month long siege.

Lieutenant General Sir Frederick Stanley Maude, battle experienced on the Western Front, and at Gallipoli, was

Right: *Riflemen of the 3rd Battalion The 3rd Gurkha Rifles, 75th Division, standing to in their trench with fixed bayonets, or possibly about to go over the top.*

GENERAL SIR EDMUND ALLENBY, COMMANDER-IN-CHIEF EGYPTIAN EXPEDITIONARY FORCE

Allenby, shown here after the war as a field marshal, was appointed Commander-in-Chief in Egypt in June 1917. Known in the British Army as "the Bull" for his great size and uncertain temper, Allenby was then a cavalry officer aged 56. Until then he had been commanding the Third Army on the Western Front under Sir Douglas Haig. The two did not get on, and Allenby thought at first that Haig had dismissed him, until Lloyd George told him that he had personally selected him for the Middle East. He did not tell him that he was the second choice, the South African General Jan Smuts having refused the offer. It turned out to be an inspired choice.

Immediately on assuming command, Allenby was told that his son had been killed in France. He was deeply affected by the news, as his private letters show, but to those around him nothing about his behaviour betrayed his emotions. His army was formed into three corps: the Desert Mounted Corps under Lieutenant General Sir Henry Chauvel, XX Corps under Lieutenant General Sir Philip Chetwode, and XXI Corps under Lieutenant General Edward Stanislaus Bulfin. Very soon the Egyptian Expeditionary Force was animated by Allenby's sense of purpose and his air of great confidence. He was to prove an outstanding commander.

sent out to take command in Mesopotamia. He brought with him three British divisions. Maude's operational methods, which included limited advances with plenty of artillery support, met with success. He retook Kut-al-Amara on 24 February 1917. Turkish resistance disintegrated, and Maude entered Baghdad on 11 March 1917. Large-scale operations ceased, but the fighting and British advance continued. Maude died of cholera in Baghdad on 18 November 1917.

PALESTINE

On 1 February 1915, the Turks attacked the Suez Canal across the Sinai desert, with the aim of advancing into Egypt and cutting Britain's line of communication to India. The Turks were thrown back with heavy losses, including large numbers who died of thirst. Eventually, in February 1916, the Commander-in-Chief in Egypt,

General Sir Archibald Murray, persuaded a half-convinced War Council in London that the best way to defend Egypt and the Canal was to occupy Sinai. Accordingly he advanced, occupying El Arish in Sinai in December 1916. Pushing on with the Australian and New Zealand Mounted Division leading, he reached Rafah on 7 January 1917. By early February Murray had constructed water pipes and a railway line to El Arish. He then proceeded to mount two attacks on Gaza. By the end of April both attacks had failed with around 10,500 British and Imperial casualties. In June, General Sir Edmund Allenby, arriving from command of the Third Army on the Western Front, replaced Murray. Despite the losses sustained in the campaign so far, the new British Prime Minister, David Lloyd George, was much taken with the idea of attacking somewhere other than on the Western Front. Accordingly Allenby's force

Below: *A squadron of the 13th Hussars crossing the Hasa Su near Kirkuk.*

THOMAS EDWARD LAWRENCE

Lawrence first worked in the Middle East in 1909 as an archaeologist in Syria after graduating from Oxford. On the outbreak of the First World War, he was commissioned and worked in the geographical section of the War Office in London. After being posted to the intelligence branch of the British headquarters in Cairo, he was sent on a mission to the Hejaz in October 1916. Here he met Sharif Hussein bin Ali of Mecca, who had raised a rebellion against the Ottomans – Arabia then being part of the Ottoman Empire. Lawrence soon became a confidant of Sharif Hussein's son, the Emir Faisal, and was appointed liaison officer with the Arabs. He arranged support for Faisal's advance up the Red Sea coast to Wej, followed by attacking the Hejaz railway the Turkish supply line. Lawrence encouraged Faisal to capture the port of Aqaba, so his Arabs could be supplied by sea, and supported in their operations against the Turkish rear and flanks, while Allenby engaged the Turkish armies.

He never claimed to be the leader of the Arab revolt, but getting to the truth about exactly where he fitted in has not been made easy by the fact that not everything he wrote is totally accurate. He was enigmatic about publicity, at one moment appearing to shun it, while "backing into the limelight". Among Arabs today he is not remembered as one of their leaders, but as a British spy with a talent for destroying trains, track and bridges.

His popularity in the interwar years, and with some people today, is possibly due to his war experience being seen as more romantic than the blood, mud and mass casualties in other First World War campaigns, the Western Front especially.

BATTLE OF BEERSHEBA – CHARGE OF THE AUSTRALIAN LIGHT HORSE

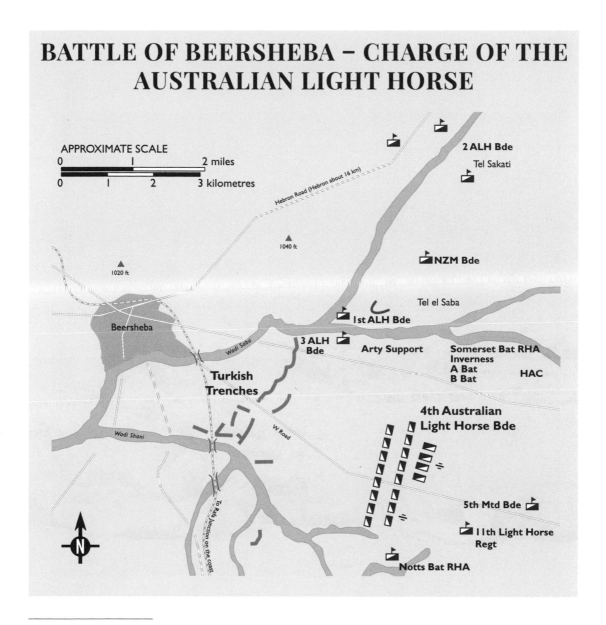

APPROXIMATE SCALE

0   1   2 miles

0   1   2   3 kilometres

Hebron Road (Hebron about 16 km)

2 ALH Bde
Tel Sakati

1040 ft

1020 ft

NZM Bde

Tel el Saba

1st ALH Bde

Beersheba

Wadi Saba

3 ALH Bde

Arty Support

Somerset Bat RHA
Inverness
A Bat
B Bat   HAC

Turkish Trenches

4th Australian Light Horse Bde

Wadi Shani

W Road

5th Mtd Bde

To Rafa Junction on the coast

11th Light Horse Regt

Notts Bat RHA

N

Top left and above: *The Australian Light Horse were mounted infantry, usually fighting dismounted, using their horses as transport to the battlefield, and a swift means of disengaging if required. Unusually, the Light Horse won the Battle of Beersheba by a cavalry charge. The Battle took place on 31 October 1917 as part of the third Battle of Gaza. The cavalry had a 36-mile approach march, and their riders knew that there was no water until they took Beersheba. By midday, three British infantry divisions had driven the Turks back from the outskirts of the town but all the wells were still in Turkish hands. Lieutenant Sir Harry Chauvel commanding the Desert Mounted Corps decided to attack the remaining enemy* trenches *with the Australian Fourth Light Horse Brigade from the south-east. Their commander, Brigadier General Grant, said to the Australian 12th Light Horse Regiment, "men you're fighting for water. There's no water between this side of Beersheba and Esani. Use your bayonets as swords. I wish you the best of luck." Normally the Light Horse would have dismounted to take the trenches, but some of 12th Light Horse went straight on at the full gallop, some jumping the trenches with Turks underneath, while the Fourth Light Horse dismounted and attacked on foot. The shock and sheer speed enabled the Light Horse Brigade to take the town for the loss of 31 dead and 36 wounded.*

Below: *Battle of Beersheba, Turkish machine gunners await the British attack on 31 October 1917.*

was increased to seven British and Imperial infantry divisions and three cavalry divisions (this cavalry force included the Australian Light Horse). This constituted the largest diversion of British troops from the Western Front in the war.

At Beersheba Allenby defeated the Turks by a massed cavalry charge, and at Gaza by artillery concentrations. Allenby captured Jerusalem, walking bareheaded into the Holy City on 9 December 1917; a welcome Christmas "present" to the British public after the many disappointing events of 1917.

Throughout 1917, the British efforts in Palestine had been assisted by the fact that the Turks were forced to divert troops to the Hejaz, where T. E. Lawrence, with Arab guerrilla forces, was cutting the railway to the Turkish garrison at Medina. The effects of Lawrence's efforts have been overplayed, although not overtly by Lawrence himself – by his own admission some of the incidents related in his book, *Seven Pillars of Wisdom*, are not strictly accurate. He did, however, meet the yardstick of a successful "special force": he tied down a great many more enemy troops than he commanded. He did not, as some romanticists claim, win the campaign almost single-handed. Without the pressure exerted by Allenby, the Turks could have turned on Lawrence and destroyed him at their leisure.

PART 4
OVERTURE TO CHANGING FORTUNES

10

NEW BRITISH TACTICS

THE GREAT BATTLES THAT LAY AHEAD FOLLOWING THE STEMMING OF THE GERMAN OFFENSIVE WERE TO SEE THE BRITISH (INCLUDING OF COURSE THE AUSTRALIANS, NEW ZEALANDERS AND CANADIANS) PUTTING TO GOOD USE THE TACTICAL LESSONS THEY HAD LEARNED IN THE PRECEDING YEARS OF THE WAR.

The first involved changes in the techniques for artillery, which meant that guns could now hit targets picked from the map or air photographs, without preliminary ranging, which gave warning of an impending attack. More accurate survey combined with air reconnaissance and photographic interpretation provided the exact location of enemy positions. Accurate counter-battery fire was made possible by sound ranging: a line of microphones picked up the sound of enemy guns and pinpointed their position. Flash-spotting was

Previous page: A gun-carrying tank – one attempt to provide mobility for the artillery in the shell-torn landscape of the Western Front.

Left: Handley Page 0/400 bomber.

Above: An Australian infantry platoon of the 29th Battalion being briefed by their platoon commander, Lieutenant Rupert Downes MC. It is only 16 strong instead of 30 or more, companies often went into battle only 50 strong instead of over 100, and battalions around 300. However, the firepower of an Australian (and British, Canadian and New Zealand) platoon, even at this reduced strength, was still greater than that of a platoon in the first three years of the war, thanks to Lewis guns (three in this platoon), and grenade launchers.

Above: *Whippet tank.*

equally important in the pinpointing of enemy guns. Other factors that contributed to greater accuracy were an understanding of how a shell was affected by barrel wear, air pressure and high altitude wind. Meteorological messages were sent to gun positions every four hours giving wind speed, direction and temperature at various altitudes. Long preliminary bombardments preceding an attack, some lasting for days, giving ample warning of the place of an impending attack, were things of the past. Now, a massive weight of fire would be brought down for a few minutes to drive defenders below ground. Next a creeping barrage would be fired, moving forward in stages, followed closely by the infantry – "leaning on the barrage" as it was called at the time. When the dazed defenders emerged, the infantry was on them with rifle, bayonet and grenade, before they had time to man their weapons.

Tanks had also improved since the earlier types used on the Somme in 1916. The new Mark V was still slow by Second World War standards; its top speed on roads 4.6 miles an hour, a fast walking pace – much slower across country, so effectively a mobile pillbox. But it was simpler to drive requiring one crew member compared

with three in earlier Marks. Some tanks were fitted with a bell inside, which was connected to a wire pull outside. This enabled infantry to attract the attention of the commander, who could open a side hatch and talk to them, enabling better co-operation between armour and infantry; an improvement on banging on the side of the tank with a rifle butt. The British now also had a medium tank, the Medium Mark A, rather misleadingly dubbed the Whippet; weighing 14 tons, with a road speed of 8.3 mph, it hardly lived up to its canine name. But with four Hotchkiss machine guns it was a valuable addition to the British capability.

In addition the British had introduced the concept of supply tanks and gun carrying tanks. The supply tank, as the name implies, was designed to bring forward supplies and principally artillery ammunition over muddy, rough ground full of shell holes. Similarly, gun-carrying tanks carried artillery pieces forward – the gun was seldom, if ever, fired from the tank. These tracked vehicles enabled the momentum of an advance to be maintained. Until their introduction, after each phase of an attack, when the advance had reached the limit of the supporting artillery, there had been long pauses while guns and ammunition were laboriously moved forward. This allowed the enemy time to bring up reserves to mount counter-attacks and to improve their defences.

As well as providing up to date information on enemy positions with air photographs, the newly formed Royal Air Force (established on 1 April 1918) supported the army by bombing and strafing enemy positions, again rudimentary by later standards, but valuable none the less. Aircraft were also used to drop ammunition to forward troops. To begin with, the drops were inaccurate but improved with practice. Aircraft were also used to fly back and forth over a sector in which formations were moving up to the line, prior to an assault, to cover the noise of tanks, artillery and their ammunition limbers and wagons.

The infantry were trained and practised in flexible tactics. Advancing in rigid lines was out. Now infantrymen advanced in "blobs", small groups of men, alternately moving and covering the other "blob", in what became known as fire and movement: one blob moving, another covering it with fire. The light machine gun, the Lewis gun, provided far greater firepower than a bolt-operated, single-shot rifle, and was invaluable for these new tactics. In addition, the infantry now had its own "mini" artillery in the form of rifle grenade launchers. These fitted on the muzzle of a rifle and, using a special cartridge, would project a grenade far further than a man could throw it. Soldiers were taught that if held up by a pillbox or strongpoint, or sometimes just a group of defenders in a shell hole, one blob was to go to

Below: *Supply tank.*

ground and return fire with Lewis gun rifles and grenade launchers, while others worked round to a flank. Trench mortars and Vickers machine guns also fired in support of the infantry.

All these innovations, and the way that artillery, infantry, tanks and air were orchestrated meant that the British Army was now fighting what today's soldiers call "an all arms battle", rudimentary at first, but improving rapidly with practice. The biggest limitation was the absence of portable battlefield radios; these would not come until the Second World War. Despite this drawback, the British Army by mid-1918 had become the best-led and best-trained army in its long history. It was about to put this training and experience into effect in a series of great successful battles, each bigger than any fought by the British Army in the Second World War.

Below: *Handley Page bombers were used to drown out the noise of tanks moving up at night before an attack.*

THE SECOND BATTLE
OF THE MARNE

**THE GERMAN OFFENSIVES COVERED IN EARLIER CHAPTERS ARE SOMETIMES
ACCLAIMED AS MASTERPIECES OF TACTICAL ART. CERTAINLY, LUDENDORFF HAD
SUCCEEDED IN SEIZING MORE GROUND IN THREE MONTHS THAN THE ALLIES
HAD GAINED IN OVER THREE YEARS OF STRIVING SINCE NOVEMBER 1914.**

Fortunately for the Allies, the Germans made no strategic gains whatsoever, at the cost of almost bringing the German Army to its knees. Between March and July, Ludendorff by creating huge salients into the Allied lines, greatly elongated the length of front he had to hold and stretched his supply lines. German casualties had been around one million. The troops released from the Eastern Front after the Russian surrender had been expended.

From the Allied perspective the offensives had come as a shock. There was panic in Paris, and French politicians began to lose their nerve, making plans to move the government to Bordeaux. But there were benefits for the Allies: the attacks forced them to unify under Foch as Allied Commander-in-Chief, and made the French and British co-operate much more readily, including moving substantial bodies of troops to each other's assistance.

Left: *Officers of the 2nd Battalion, King's Own Yorkshire Light Infantry, 62nd Division, conferring with French and Italian officers in the Bois de Reims during the Battle of Tardenois, 24 July 1918.*

Above: *A German MG 08 machine gun section advancing to take up new positions in the ruins of a house on the Montdidier – Noyon sector of the front, June 1918.*

Above: *The Battle of Tardenois. Men of the 2nd Battalion, King's Own Yorkshire Light Infantry, 62nd Division, examining a captured German Maxim 08/15 (Spandau) machine gun with French and Italian officers. Bois de Reims, 24 July 1918.*

From mid-June 1918 there was stalemate on the Western Front until 15 July, when the Germans, trying yet again, mounted a major offensive on the Marne. There was no tactical surprise. The German techniques were now well understood. Allied aircrews knew what to look for, how to recognize the signs heralding an attack. The German air force, outnumbered and short of fuel, was unable to keep the skies clear of Allied reconnaissance aircraft.

The Germans planned to open the second battle of the Marne with a bombardment at 10 minutes after midnight on 14/15 July. The alert French evacuated their front lines before the German barrage started. French counter-battery fire hit the German gun lines before they started their own bombardment programme. About four

hours later the French gunners switched targets to hit the German infantry moving forward. Along much of the attack frontage, the Germans could not penetrate the French Forward Zone. In places where they did, they were halted on the Second Line by Allied reserves.

The Allied counter-offensive began on the Marne. On 18 July, four French Armies accompanied by 750 tanks attacked from left to right – the Tenth, Sixth, Ninth and Fifth. The French offensive began with the Tenth and Sixth Armies attacking the western flank of the German bulge. As the Germans fell back, the Ninth and Fifth came into play on the nose of the bulge and its eastern flank. The German retreat gathered momentum and by 7 August they were back on the Aisne. General Charles Mangin's French Tenth Army had performed especially

THE LAST GERMAN OFFENSIVE, JULY 1918

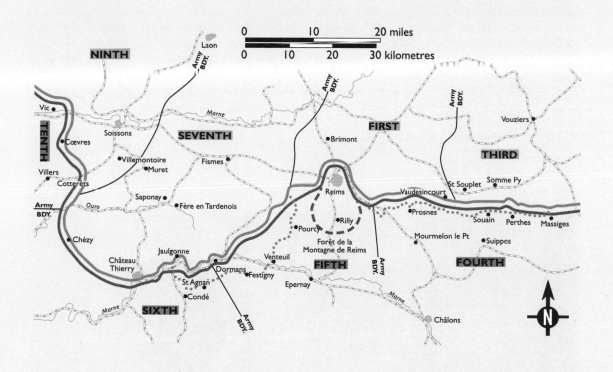

NINTH

Laon

0   10   20 miles
0   10   20   30 kilometres

Vic

TENTH

Cœvres

Soissons

SEVENTH

Marne

Brimont

FIRST

Army BDY.

Vouziers

Villers

Villemontoire

Muret

Fismes

THIRD

Cotterèts

Saponay

Fère en Tardenois

St Souplet

Somme Py

Army BDY.

Ouro

Reims

Vaudesincourt

Prosnes

Souain

Perthes

Massiges

Chézy

Jaulgonne

Pourcy

Rilly

Château Thierry

Venteuil

Dormans

Forêt de la Montagne de Reims

Mourmelon le Pt

Suippes

FOURTH

St Agnan

Festigny

FIFTH

Army BDY.

Condé

SIXTH

Epernay

Marne

Châlons

Army BDY.

Marne

N

———— German front line on 15 July
••••••••• German front line on 17 July

———— French front line on 15 July
– – – – French defences of Reims on 15 July

well. Attached to the French XX Corps in Mangin's army were the 1st and 2nd US Divisions, who acquitted themselves well, most notable of all being the feats of the US Marine Brigade in the US 2nd Division at Soissons just south of the Aisne.

Ludendorff dropped any notions of an attack on the British in Flanders and directed his attention to the crisis further south. Here he found the French offensive had halted. Most of the French tanks were destroyed or badly in need of repair and maintenance. The infantry was drained and German reserves had managed to stabilize the line. The Second Battle of the Marne was over. Between 15 July and 5 August the French armies and Allied formations with them had taken nearly 30,000 prisoners, captured 798 guns and suffered 95,000 casualties. All the Germans could hope for was a return to the siege warfare stalemate that had existed from November 1914 to 21 March 1918.

The scene on the Allied side was much more promising. The BEF had taken a hammering, but was not broken. Reinforcements were now flooding in and quickly assimilated. Perhaps most encouraging to the war-weary Allies, the number of American troops arriving in France had now risen dramatically. By the end of September 1918, 39 US divisions would arrive, each twice the size of a British or French division.

British industry was now producing weapons and munitions in massive quantities. In Germany, thanks to the Royal Navy's blockade, industry was in steep decline. This and breakdowns in the rail system resulting in a coal shortage in factories meant that manufacturers were unable to meet the demands of the German Army. When the Allies went on the offensive and captured weapons, they could not be replaced.

While the French drew breath, Foch made it clear to the British that it was now their turn.

GENERAL CHARLES MANGIN

Known as the "butcher" and "eater of men", Mangin spent his early years in the French African colonies and was a fervent admirer of African troops to whom he had entrusted some of the more daunting tasks at the Battle of Verdun in 1916. He first came to notice at the Battle of Charleroi in August 1914. At Verdun he rose from divisional command to lead the Third Army in a series of successful counter-attacks in late 1916. Very brave, he took enormous personal risks and was wounded several times. Sacked after the abortive 1917 Nivelle offensive, he was brought back to command the 10th Army in the summer of 1918. His aggressive spirit and personal leadership played a major part in reinvigorating the French Army after the mutinies of 1917. His talents were given full play in the Second Battle of the Marne. Mangin advanced six miles, taking 15,000 prisoners and 400 guns. He continued to command successfully for the rest of the war, still hated by his soldiers.

THE SECOND BATTLE OF MARNE: SHOWING AMERICAN INVOLVEMENT 18 JULY–6 AUGUST 1918

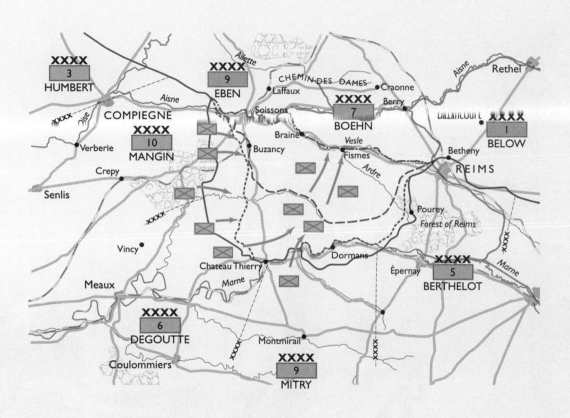

Front lines —— 18 July --- 28 July →→ American advance
----- 20 July -·-· 6 August

Next page: *German gunners and a 7.7-cm gun in the Champagne.*

LE HAMEL

ALTHOUGH THE FRENCH, AUSTRALIANS, CANADIANS, BRITISH AND AMERICANS HAD BEEN ENGAGED IN OPERATIONS IN JULY, ONE BATTLE EARLY THAT MONTH, PLANNED BY THE AUSTRALIAN CORPS COMMANDER, IS WORTHY OF ATTENTION AS FORERUNNER FOR THE MANNER IN WHICH THE BRITISH, AUSTRALIAN AND CANADIANS ESPECIALLY WERE TO FIGHT.

This notable, yet relatively unknown, battle was Le Hamel, and the harbinger, Lieutenant General John Monash's Australian Corps. Since 1916 the Australians had established an enviable record of success on the Western Front. Success in local operations in the area of Albert on the Somme had shown that the Germans were vulnerable to penetration attacks. Monash accordingly submitted a plan to Henry Rawlinson, commanding the Fourth Army, to recapture the village of Le Hamel, and Vaire and Hamel Woods. Monash believed in meticulous planning. He envisioned a battle plan as the score for an orchestral composition.

Hamel was garrisoned by the 13th, 15th, and 55th Infantry Regiments of the 13th German Division. Ten Australian battalions took part, plus five companies of tanks (60 total) of the 5th Tank Brigade plus three squadrons of Australian aircraft, as well as fighter-ground support by the RAF. The attack was to be carried out by the Australian 4th Division (Major General Ewen Sinclair-Maclagan), using only the 4th Brigade from his own division, along with the 11th Australian Brigade of the 3rd Australian Division on the left, and on the right two battalions of the 6th Brigade of the 2nd Australian Division. A total of 326 field guns and 302 heavies were

Left: *A German machine gun captured at a house in Hamel.*

Above: *Le Hamel village.*

Above: *American troops resting by the roadside on their way to join the Australians for the Battle of le Hamel.*

LIEUTENANT GENERAL SIR JOHN MONASH

Monash was a civil engineer by profession, and a part-time soldier in the Australian militia. He joined the Melbourne University Company of the Fourth Battalion Victoria Rifles before the war. He studied the military profession with as much thoroughness as a regular, and by 1913 took command of 13th Infantry Brigade as a Colonel. He landed at Gallipoli in April 1915 with his brigade, and by July had been promoted to Brigadier General. In 1916 he formed the 3rd Australian Division in England and on 7 June 1917 his division was successful in its first battle, Messines. In October his division suffered heavily at Passchendaele. On 27 March 1918, his division successfully blocked the German advance between the Somme and the Ancre. In May 1918 he was promoted to Lieutenant General to command the Australian Corps. He is pictured here as a Colonel.

LE HAMEL BATTLE

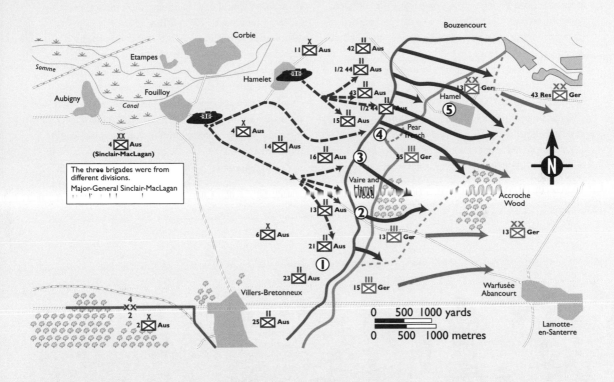

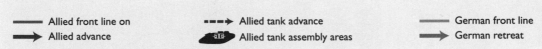

Allied front line on   Allied tank advance   German front line

Allied advance   Allied tank assembly areas   German retreat

The numbers on the map do not indicate the order in which events took place, as all three brigades attacked at the same time, but it is convenient to describe the action as follows:

① The 23rd and 21st Battalions encountered no serious opposition, and reached their objectives with slight casualties at 0449 hours.

② In the 4th Australian Brigade, the 13th Battalion had the task of passing south of Vaire wood on a narrow frontage and then opening out rapidly to cover 1200 yards of the final objective. The 13th Battalion reached its final objective at 0418 hours.

③ The 16th Battalion's job was to clear Vaire and Hamel Woods to ensure that battalions on either side were not delayed by enfilade fire. The woods were cleared in an hour and a half.

④ The 15th Battalion had more trouble. The first lift of the barrage left the salient of Pear Trench clear, and the Germans had time to man their machine guns before the first wave reached the uncut wire. The wire was finally cut, but it was only after a fierce fight with the bayonet that Pear Trench was taken. By 0700 hours the battalion was well dug in on its objective.

⑤ The 11th Brigade with its tanks and American contingent had to capture Hamel and beyond the village re-establish the old French line, which ran down to the River Somme, east of Bouzencourt. The brigade kicked off with the 42nd and 43rd Battalions in the lead. On reaching their intermediate halt line after encountering little opposition, except fire from Pear Trench, the 44th Battalion, "leap-frogged" the 43rd, and resuming the advance, divided into two, one half moving south and the other, north of Hamel, each supported by six tanks. The 43rd with the six remaining tanks cleared the village. The final objective was reached between 0445 and 0455 hours. Mopping up of Hamel caused little trouble, and the enemy – surprised in deep dugouts – surrendered quickly.

in support. In addition, 147 machine guns from five Australian machine-gun battalions would fire in support. American troops were attached to gain battle experience as follows: 13th Battalion, one company; 15th Battalion, one company; and 11th Brigade, two companies. Coincidentally, the attack was to be carried out on 4 July, American Independence Day.

The attack would be preceded by a creeping barrage, followed by infantry and tanks working together. The Australians had bitter memories of being let down by tanks at Bullecourt the year before and initially were sceptical about them. But these were Mark V tanks, a greatly improved model over the Mark IIs at Bullecourt. No wire cutting would be carried out by the artillery; this would be left to the tanks and the infantry.

RAF aircraft were to drop resupplies of ammunition by parachute to troops on the ground and supply tanks were to carry more ammunition and other stores; to carry these stores would have required 1,250 men as porters.

Zero Hour was 0310 on 4 July 1918, one hour and 32 minutes before sunrise. The artillery preparation included laying down smoke. For some days before the battle, Monash had mixed gas with smoke in his bombardments, so that the Germans when they saw smoke immediately put on their gas masks, making it more difficult to fight. On this occasion there was no gas mixed in; the Australians did not wear their masks, but the Germans did.

At 2230 hours on 3 July, the tanks moved up from their assembly positions under the cover of noise from

aircraft flying along the whole of the Fourth Army front and positioned themselves about 1,000 yards behind the tapes from which the infantry were to begin the advance. For several nights before the operation, aircraft flew these sorties to accustom the Germans to this activity.

As the barrage opened on the Germans, the tanks moved to join the infantry, using the noise from the artillery to cover the sound of their movement. The stages of the battle are shown on the accompanying map (page 107).

The battle went so smoothly and exactly as planned, and it was all over in 93 minutes. Covered by a thick ground mist, the Australians and Americans speedily secured their objectives, taking 1,472 prisoners, two guns, 171 machine guns and 41 mortars, for 775 Australian and 134 American casualties (dead, wounded and missing). Among the long list of engagements in the First World War, Le Hamel is a small battle few people will have heard of, yet its significance as a signpost to the way ahead was enormous. It was a masterpiece, and Haig's headquarters published the battle plan as a brochure for the edification of the whole BEF. It stressed the importance of meticulous planning and the need for cooperation between infantry, artillery, machine-gunners, tanks and the RAF. It provided a model for how the BEF as a whole would conduct its attacks in future.

Below: *German prisoners captured in the fighting at Hamel, congregated near the 4th Australian Infantry Brigade Headquarters in a quarry just south of Corbie, prior to their removal to a compound (the "bird cage").*

13

THE ALLIES PLAN TO ROLL THE GERMANS BACK

ON 24 JULY 1918, AN IMPORTANT CONFERENCE WAS HELD AT GENERAL FOCH'S NEW HEADQUARTERS AT BOMBON CHÂTEAU, SOUTH EAST OF PARIS. PRESENT WERE: GENERALS FOCH, PÉTAIN, HAIG, AND PERSHING, ALONG WITH OTHER COMMANDERS AND THEIR STAFFS.

The proceedings opened with General Maxime Weygand, Foch's Chief of Staff, reading out Foch's memorandum which was to form the basis of future Allied action. It began by saying: "The fifth German offensive, checked at the outset, has been a failure from the very start. The offensive by the French Tenth and Sixth Armies has turned that failure into defeat. This must be exploited to the full ..."

Foch now intended to pass from the defensive to the offensive in a series of operations carried out at short intervals so that the enemy would not have time to move reserves and supplies to meet the new threat. In effect what Foch proposed was raining a succession of blows on the enemy, in different places along the front. When one offensive had gained its objective, and while the enemy was still engrossed in countering it, and taking steps to prevent further Allied exploitation in that sector, another Allied offensive would be mounted almost immediately somewhere else. Foch was to demonstrate that the way to attack a continuous fortified line was by this method rather than several simultaneous assaults, or one big "push". These

attacks would include operations east of Amiens by Haig's BEF, and in the St Mihiel sector by Pershing's Americans. Pershing later wrote: "the conference decidedly confirmed the principle of co-operation and emphasized the wisdom of having a co-ordinating head for the Allied forces."

On 28 July, Weygand handed Haig a directive from Foch giving him command of the French First Army and his mission contained a *directive particulière* or "special directive". It said:

1. The object of the operation is to disengage Amiens and the Paris–Amiens railway, also to defeat and drive back the enemy established between the Somme and the Avre.
2. To do so the offensive covered on the north by the Somme will push as far as possible in the direction of the Roye.
3. It will be executed by:
   (i) The British Fourth Army, composed at the start of 12 divisions and three cavalry divisions, supported by
   (ii) The French First Army reinforced by four divisions.

Below: *American troops landing at Havre, 12 July 1918.*

The date set for Haig's operation was 8 August 1918, which was to become the turning point of the First World War.

On the "other side of the hill", in Germany, the mood was less upbeat. Despite a closely controlled press, the newspapers were printing comments such as: "the hour has come when the faith of the nation in the future and in victory requires to be sustained with a strong heart", and "it is the resistance of the nerves that will win the War". There was mention of "a serious moral depression". There was little mention, however, of the heavy cost of the German offensives in France, the failure of unrestricted submarine warfare, and the arrival of American troops in France. To dwell on the last two topics would merely serve to illustrate the strategic ineptitude of the actual leaders of Germany – Ludendorff and Hindenburg – because the entry of the United States on the Entente side in the War owed a great deal to the decision to engage in unrestricted submarine warfare.

Meanwhile Ludendorff drew up an appreciation of the situation on 2 August, which included the need to "resume the offensive as soon as possible". The places

Below: *Americans in French Renault tanks. The Americans had no tanks of their own.*

Above: *American Officers at rifle grenade and bombing practice at British XI Corps School.*

where the German Army was to plan attacks were listed. He also attempted to predict where the Allied blows would fall. He failed to include most of the Amiens sector.

On 7 August, Foch, about to be created a Marshal of France on 9 August, issued an order of the day to his French armies. It concluded:

Four years of effort aided by our faithful Allies, four years of trial stoically accepted, commence to bear their fruit.

Broken in his fifth attempt in 1918, the invader has recoiled. His effectives [sic] are failing, his morale is weakening, whilst on our side, our American comrades, just disembarked, have already made our disconcerted enemy feel the vigour of their blows.

Yesterday I said to you: Obstinacy, Patience, your American comrades are coming. Today I say to you: Tenacity, Boldness, and Victory must be yours.

PART 5
THE BATTLE OF AMIENS

14

BATTLE OF AMIENS: PREPARING

THE PREPARATIONS FOR THE BATTLE OF AMIENS BY RAWLINSON'S BRITISH FOURTH ARMY WERE MADE DIFFICULT BY LACK OF TIME, THE NUMEROUS MOVES THAT WERE NECESSARY BEFOREHAND, AND THE NEED TO CONCEAL THE PREPARATIONS FROM THE GERMANS.

The Canadian Corps had to be moved south from Flanders and positioned between the French and the Australians. The British III Corps had to take over the section of the Australian line north of the Somme, while the Cavalry Corps and 1st Australian Division had to move to new locations. As well as moving troops and equipment, the logistical demands were huge. For example the Canadian Corps alone required 70,000 tons of artillery shells and 10 million rounds of small arms ammunition. The Fourth Army ammunition dumps were so far back that a truck could make only one trip a day from these to the forward gun lines. Traffic congestion on the only two roads forward was a further limitation, especially since the Canadians and Australians shared them. All the while the soldiers had to be fed and watered, thousands of horses and mules likewise (with bulky fodder), and trucks kept filled with petrol. Although the BEF was well supplied with trucks, much of the artillery relied on horses and mules to tow guns and carry supplies, as did infantry divisions and most parts of the army. This was not because of the whims of horse-obsessed "cavalry generals" as the mythmakers would have it. The trucks of the time, with solid rubber tyres and without four-wheel drive, were almost useless across country, and were easily bogged down on muddy

roads. Only horses, mules and the relatively few tracked vehicles could cope off-road. To this end, five supply tank companies, and two gun carrier tank companies, were attached to the Fourth Army.

The railways were crucial. Nearly every railhead in the Fourth Army's sector had been overrun in the great German March push. New lines had to be laid, and this was achieved in the early summer. It was also vital to preserve secrecy, especially about the move of the Canadians. The Canadian Corps, by agreement between their government and Britain's, would only fight as a Corps (all four divisions as one). The move of a complete, elite corps all the way from Flanders to the Somme would signal Rawlinson's intent to the Germans. The security measures to conceal these preparations included telling all officers in the Canadian Corps that anyone, anywhere detected talking about an offensive would be arrested and court-martialled, regardless of his rank.

All these preparations, including the production of complex marching, road and rail movement tables, artillery fire support plans, and the collection and collation of intelligence, required meticulous work by the staffs at corps, division and brigade: the "red tabs", the butt of many jokes, but without whom nothing could be achieved.

Previous page: Trucks bringing forward supplies. In 1914 the BEF had 334 trucks, and by 1918 the number had risen to 33,560.

Left: Standard gauge railway line being laid, advancing about a mile a day.

Above: *A Bristol Fighter of Number 22 Squadron "banking" (taken from another machine). Serny aerodrome, 17 June 1918.*

LIEUTENANT GENERAL SIR ARTHUR CURRIE

At the start of the First World War, Arthur Currie was an estate agent and part-time soldier commanding a militia battalion in Canada, but was soon chosen to command the Canadian 2nd Infantry Brigade. He had also stolen $11,000 from regimental funds to cover losses incurred while speculating in gold. Fortunately for him, when his crime was discovered he had powerful friends who enabled him to remain in command. Currie was a gambler but also one of those rare people: a born soldier. He did not look like one, pear shaped and weighing 108 kg (17 stone) with a bulging stomach. On 22 April 1915 he distinguished himself during the first gas attack at the Second Battle of Ypres. He commanded the Canadian 2nd Division at the Somme and at Vimy Ridge, and was appointed to command the Canadian Corps in April 1917, becoming the first Canadian Lieutenant General. At Passchendaele during the Third Battle of Ypres, his Corps captured the ridge with fewer casualties than predicted.

GENERAL SIR HENRY RAWLINSON

Rawlinson first saw action as a Lieutenant in Burma in 1886. He served on Lord Kitchener's staff during the campaign in the Sudan in 1898. He served with distinction in the Second Boer War from 1899 to 1902. He commanded the 4th Division in France in 1914 before taking command of IV Corps. In 1915 his Corps led all the attacks in Haig's First Army, and he was promoted to command Fourth Army in February 1916. At the Battle of the Somme he favoured "bite and hold" attacks, but Haig overruled him. His piecemeal attacks in July and August 1916, with inadequate forces on narrow frontages, were costly. Sidelined for most of 1917 in favour of Hubert Gough's Fifth Army the Fourth Army was used to reinforce the rest of the BEF during the Ypres battles and was effectively disbanded. When Gough was relieved of command of Fifth Army, Rawlinson took over. Fifth Army was renamed Fourth Army shortly afterwards, with XIX Corps remaining in being during this process.

The attack was to be supported by nine tank battalions. The tanks moved forward to their pre-assault areas at night. The noise was covered by aircraft flying overhead. Thanks to the Le Hamel operation the Australians had gained confidence in tank support, but more training with tanks was deemed necessary and carried out over a specially prepared piece of ground made to look as near to a battleground as possible, with wire, trenches and shell holes: more work for the staffs.

Man-portable battlefield radios did not appear in any army until the Second World War. To maintain the momentum of the attack it was vital for commanders and their staffs at all levels to know how the battle was progressing and give orders for subsequent action. If the advance was rapid there would be no time to lay or bury telephone lines (unburied lines would be cut by shellfire, tanks and gun and limber wheels). Pigeons and mounted messengers were to be used to communicate situation reports and orders. The RAF was tasked with reporting on progress. Specially allocated army co-operation aircraft were fitted with coloured streamers and had their wings and fuselages painted to show which formation they were working with. The troops on the ground, seeing one of their allocated aircraft overhead, displayed coloured panels and fired flares to indicate their location, or to call for artillery support on pre-planned targets (usually the one that was the most threatening, called "the SOS target").

As well as the six-army co-operation squadrons, the RAF also provided 28 fighter and bomber squadrons. The day and night bomber squadrons would hit key German rail centres to slow down and even stop the move forward of reserves. The fighters would escort the day bombers, and provide what modern soldiers call close air support to the soldiers. Two squadrons would be tasked with laying smokescreens for the Australians and Canadians. One of these squadrons would also drop machine gun ammunition by parachute to III Corps and the Australians.

This was the first time that John Monash's Australian Corps was to fight together as one formation, and in his order of the day, read out to all his men, he pointed this out, saying that all the operations of the previous four months had been in preparation for the forthcoming great effort. Having expressed his confidence in them he concluded: "I earnestly wish every soldier in the Corps the best of good fortune, and glorious and decisive victory the story of which will re-echo throughout the world, and will live forever in the history of our homeland."

Below: *A squadron of Royal Aircraft Factory F.E.2b night bombers lined up on Aire Aerodrome, 19 January 1918.*

15

AMIENS, 8 AUGUST 1918
– THE OBJECTIVES

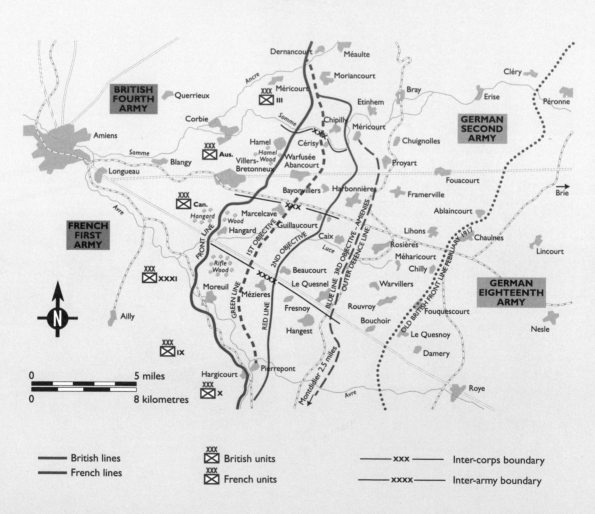

Dernancourt
Méaulte
Morlancourt
Cléry
Erise
Péronne

Ancre
BRITISH FOURTH ARMY
Querrieux
XXX III Méricourt
Bray
Chipilly
Etinhem
Méricourt

Corbie
Somme
Chuignolles
GERMAN SECOND ARMY
Amiens
Somme
Hamel
Cérisy
Proyart

Blangy
XXX Aus.
Hamel Wood
Warfusée Abancourt

Longueau
Villers-Bretonneux
Bayonvillers
Harbonnières
Framerville
Fouacourt
Brie

Avre
XXX Can.
Marcelcave
XXX
Ablaincourt

FRENCH FIRST ARMY
Hangard Wood
Guillaucourt
Lihons

Hangard
Caix
Rosières
Chaulnes
Lincourt

Luce
Méharicourt
GERMAN EIGHTEENTH ARMY

XXX XXXI
Rifle Wood
Beaucourt
Chilly

Moreuil
Mézières
XXXX
Le Quesnel
Warvillers

Ailly
Fresnoy
Rouvroy
Fouquescourt
Nesle

XXX IX
Hangest
Bouchoir
Le Quesnoy

Damery

Hargicourt
Pierrepont
Montdidier 2.5 miles
Avre
Roye

XXX X

N

| 0 | | 5 miles |
| 0 | | 8 kilometres |

FRONT LINE
1ST OBJECTIVE
2ND OBJECTIVE
3RD OBJECTIVE – AMIENS
OUTER DEFENCE LINE
BLUE LINE
GREEN LINE
RED LINE
OLD BRITISH FRONT LINE FEBRUARY 1917

| | British lines | XXX ⊠ British units | ——— XXX ——— | Inter-corps boundary |
| | French lines | XXX ⊠ French units | ——— XXXX ——— | Inter-army boundary |

BATTLE OF AMIENS: FIRST DAY – BRITISH III CORPS

DESPITE THE MANY DIFFICULTIES THAT HAD TO BE OVERCOME TO PREPARE FOR THE GREAT OFFENSIVE, ALL WAS NOW READY.

On the night of 7/8 August 1918, General Rawlinson wrote in his diary:

There is nothing to show that the Bosche knows what is coming S [sic – south] of the Somme. We shall have eight excellent Divns [sic] and 350 tanks against him, and three Divns of Cavy [sic – Cavalry] ready to pass through any hole that is made. I have great hopes that we may win a big success.

At about 3.00 am on 8 August, ground mist began to creep along the river valleys, and spreading to the higher ground, thickened at the approach of dawn. It meant that the RAF co-operation was restricted, and some assaulting troops would have difficulty navigating to their objectives. But the bad visibility disadvantaged the defenders even more. This time it was the British who would attack under the cover of mist, which would not clear until 10.00 am, or even later in some places. At 4.20 am – Zero Hour – the barrage came crashing down. An Australian wrote after the war: "the gigantic orchestra of 680 guns crashed into the opening bar of the overture of the 'Battle of the Hundred Days'. The assaulting troops began to move forward just three minutes after the barrage began."

Rawlinson's diary entry does not mention attacks north of the Somme; perhaps because the major blow was to be delivered south of the river. However, his army was also to attack north of the Somme, in the shape of British III Corps whose three divisions (12th, 18th, and 58th) had objectives between Morlancourt and the River Somme. The 18th and 58th Divisions would move off at Zero Hour, followed two hours later by the 12th Division on the left of the other two. Once the Green Line had been reached, there would be a pause of one hour to allow fresh brigades to pass through on to the Red Line. The vital ground in III Corps's sector was the Chipilly spur, the site for German guns that threatened the Australians south of the Somme. The terrain adjacent to the River Somme in this zone consisted of steep ridges, chalk riverbanks, and in some places small cliffs.

The attack began well. Despite the mist thickening with the approach of daylight, which made maintaining the axis of advance difficult, the Green Line was secured.

But thereafter, the brigades of the 58th Division became intermingled, and as a result the Chipilly spur remained in enemy hands. From here German machine-gunners could fire on the Australians advancing south of the Somme.

To the left of the 58th Division, the 18th Division's objective was to secure that part of the ridge that ran between the villages of Corbie and Bray within the III Corps's boundaries. The enemy was holding short lengths of trenches, and there was practically no barbed wire. But in the mist, it was difficult to locate these trenches and one officer likened it to a mixture of hide-and-seek and blind man's bluff. One battalion, the 7th Queens (Royal West Surrey), was held up by machine guns. Their commanding officer Lieutenant Colonel Christopher Bushell came forward and led the battalion in a successful attack on these guns. He was mortally wounded. He

had already been awarded the Victoria Cross for his outstanding leadership of the Seventh Queens, and had only just returned to his battalion after recovering from a wound.

Renewed attempts to clear the Chipilly spur were unsuccessful. More encouraging, initially, was the experience of 10th Battalion of the Essex Regiment, using the Bray–Corbie road to maintain direction. The fog suddenly lifted to reveal, right in front of the 10th Essex, two German artillery batteries with their crews all relaxing behind the gun line. The 10th Essex immediately charged and captured every man. The 10th Essex were soon joined by the 7th Royal West Kents who had also used the Bray–Corbie road to keep on course, and together they formed the left flank of the III Corps sector. But German counter-attacks drove them back to the Green Line.

Below: *60-pdr guns in action during the Battle of Amiens.*

AMIENS – DEPLOYMENT OF DIVISIONS, 8 AUGUST 1918

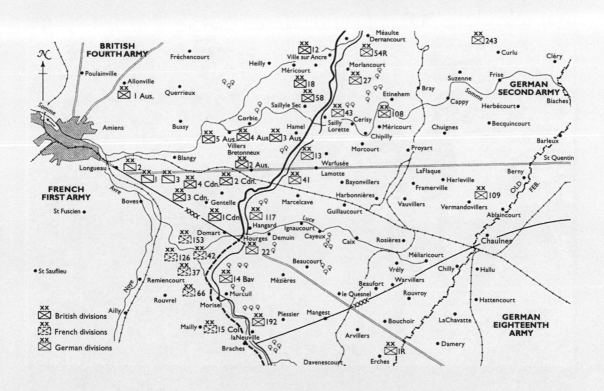

Left: *Mark V tank (crew number J44) of 10th Battalion, Tank Corps which took part in the Battle of Amiens with the III Corps.*

Above: *Tanks passing through Australian troops on the Green Line, Battle of Amiens.*

As they withdrew, only 15 men of the Royal West Kents reached it.

The objective of the follow-up attack by the 12th Division, on the extreme left of III Corps, was the spur immediately north of Morlancourt. After the second attempt, the objective was eventually secured. But the III Corps had not advanced beyond its first objective, the Green Line. The British Official History attributes this to lack of experienced company commanders,

and to the fact that many of the soldiers, especially reinforcements, had had insufficient training. To be successful when fighting in bad visibility, such as darkness, or in this case fog, requires a high standard of junior leadership, down to platoon and section commanders, and that every soldier has well developed battle skills, coupled with initiative. These were attributes the Australians and Canadians were to show in full measure.

Right: *German prisoners just captured and hurrying to the rear under escort, fearful of being hit by their own artillery.*

16

BATTLE OF AMIENS: FIRST DAY – AUSTRALIAN CORPS

WITH A ZERO HOUR OF 4.20 AM, THE AUSTRALIAN CORPS PLAN WAS TO ASSAULT WITH TWO DIVISIONS UP: THE 3RD AUSTRALIAN DIVISION IN THE NORTH AND THE 2ND AUSTRALIAN DIVISION, IN THE SOUTH.

On reaching the Green Line, at Zero plus two hours (6.20 am), both these divisions would reorganize and consolidate. Once the Green Line was securely held, the 4th and 5th Australian Divisions would pass through and advance to the Red Line, beginning at Zero plus four hours, then pressing on and securing the Blue Line. The 5th Tank Brigade – consisting of four tank battalions (Mark V and Mark V star), and one armoured car battalion – was in support of the Australians. Gun carrier tanks and supply tanks would be loaded with supplies to support both infantry and tanks.

A typical Australian brigade attack formation for the Battle of Amiens 8 on August 1918 is shown in the sketch on the next page (in this case the four battalions of 15th Australian Brigade). On encountering enemy, company column would deploy in platoon attack formation and advance in "blobs" using fire and movement supported by tanks. This formation is radically different from that used earlier in the war – infantry in line abreast along the whole sector of the attack. Company columns do not advance in a close block formation as if on parade, but in loose files of men with intervals in between, sometimes called

"artillery formation", so that one enemy shell will not wipe out a complete platoon, or even section. The position of battalion (Bn) headquarters, shown here behind all four rifle companies, could vary according to how the commanding officer of the battalion wishes to exercise control of the battle, and so he will move his HQ accordingly; for example just behind his leading two companies, or even up between them.

At Zero minus one hour, aircraft began flying over the Australian sector to cover the noise of tanks moving to the start line. The tanks waited until Zero minus 30 minutes before starting their engines and motoring forward in column, and deploying on the start line, in line, abreast. At Zero, preceded by scouts on foot to point out machine-gun posts, the tanks crossed the start line, followed by the infantry battalions in columns of companies. The inset overleaf shows the typical attack formation of an Australian brigade. By the time the barrage made its first lift at Zero plus three minutes the tanks had to be ahead of the infantry, except the scouts, and keep motoring to follow the barrage in its successive lifts. The fog made this difficult, but the tanks managed to keep station helped by officers with compasses. The latter had to dismount from their tank,

---

Left: *A tank moving forward, passing German prisoners carrying a wounded man on a stretcher.*

AUSTRALIAN BRIGADE ATTACK FORMATION

Scouts
Tanks

59th Battalion

Section
13th Light Horse
Section
14th Field Company

Bn.☐ Headquarters
☐ Section
1st Cyclist
Battalion

Scouts
Tanks

57th Battalion

Section
13th Light Horse
Section
14th Field Company

Bn.☐ Headquarters
☐ Section
1st Cyclist
Battalion

15th Light Trench Mortar battery

58th Battalion

Section
13th Light Horse

Bn.☐ Headquarters
☐ Section
1st Cyclist
Battalion

60th Battalion

Section of
13th Light Horse

Bn.☐ Headquarters
☐ Section
1st Cyclist
Battalion

15th Machine Gun Company

Hotchkiss Gun
Section of
13th Light Horse
(Anti-Aircraft)

Exploiting Detachment
in Mark V* tanks

Supply Tanks

Above: *Lieutenant Arnold's tank "Musical Box". Photographed the day after the first day of battle and being used as a collecting point for the wounded.*

and move a short distance away, to check the bearing. The steel tank affected the magnetized compass pointer, giving a false reading.

Each brigade was supported by machine guns, some of which moved with it to be ready to provide supporting fire as part of the consolidation phase of each advance. The remaining machine guns laid down a barrage at Zero Hour. Vickers machine guns could fire at pre-determined targets out to a range of 3,700 yards in darkness, or bad visibility caused by fog or smoke. A company of eight guns could lay down a devastating rain of bullets over what was known as the "beaten zone" – an oval-shaped area over 100 yards long and correspondingly wide. The artillery in support of each brigade was deployed in groups, one firing and the other moving forward to the next position. Once this was secured, and the guns were in action, the supporting group would come out of action ready to leapfrog the in-action group and move forward again.

The barrage began on time and the attackers advanced as the artillery lifted on to the next target. By 8.00 am both leading divisions were on the Green Line. The second phase of the attack began at 8.20 am, with the 4th and 5th Australian Divisions passing through the 3rd and 2nd. Each of the leading brigades in 4th and 5th Divisions had "exploiting detachments" consisting of Vickers and Lewis guns with their crews mounted on tanks. Their task was to press on through the Red Line to the Blue Line and establish strong points with tanks and both medium and light machine gun detachments. Here they would await the arrival of the main body of infantry of the brigade.

Also attached to each brigade were detachments of light mortars, engineers, cyclists and Australian Light Horse cavalry. So constituted, they were "brigade groups". As such these were the harbingers of a method of fighting that would become the norm in the Second

World War, just over 20 years later. Each division also had cavalry, armoured cars and Whippet tanks attached.

The leading brigades of the second phase of the Australian Corps attack aimed to cross the Green Line at 8.20 am. On reaching the Red Line the exploiting detachments, moving at the rear, would pass through and head for the Blue Line, followed as soon as possible by the main bodies of each brigade. The Whippets had a very good day. They found it difficult to keep up with the cavalry and, lacking radios, communications were difficult. One Whippet, nicknamed "Musical Box", had a very busy time, which only became known about after the war, as its crew, commanded by Lieutenant Clement Broomhall Arnold, were taken prisoner. Having overcome an artillery battery by attacking from the rear, he drove off some Germans engaging a cavalry patrol, and he then fired on German infantry in some huts between Bayonvilliers and Harbonnières. Arnold pressed on and beat up some wagon lines, well beyond the Blue Line. At this point the Whippet came under intense machine-gun fire and petrol leaking from the tank caught fire. The crew abandoned the tank. The driver was killed, with Arnold and Private Christopher Ribbans being taken prisoner.

By 10.30 am the Red Line was secure. By 1.30 pm the Australians were firm on the Blue Line, and had secured all their objectives, except on their extreme left flank where British III Corps had failed to take the Chipilly Ridge, thus allowing enemy machine guns to fire on the Australians. The Australians summed up their magnificent effort: "It was a très bon stunt."

Right: *German prisoners taken by the Australian Corps.*

17

BATTLE OF AMIENS: FIRST DAY – CANADIAN CORPS

LIEUTENANT GENERAL SIR ARTHUR CURRIE'S CANADIAN CORPS STARTED ITS ATTACK WITH THE SAME ZERO HOUR AS EVERYBODY ELSE IN FOURTH ARMY – AT 4.20 AM ON 8 AUGUST.

The French, on the right of the Canadians, were due to cross their start line an hour later. The Canadians, starting at the "bulge" of a salient (see map, p.124) had further to go to reach the final objective than anyone else. Currie decided to assault with three of his four divisions up, with 4th Division starting from a position about four miles behind, passing through later. To cope with the likelihood of a gap opening up between his right flank and the French as he advanced, Currie, in his usual innovative fashion, created an Independent Force, under Brigadier-General Raymond Brutinel. It consisted of 1st and 2nd Canadian Motor Machine Gun Brigades, the Canadian Cyclist Battalion, and one section of medium trench mortars mounted on trucks. The task of this force was to pass through the 3rd Canadian Division, and assure flank protection by clearing the Amiens–Roye road between the Red and Blue Lines. The force was also tasked to support the cavalry, should they be able to push beyond the Blue Line. The force kept mainly to the old Roman Road from Amiens to Roye, because the cross-country mobility of their motor transport was so limited.

The Canadians had secured the Green Line by

7.45 am and the Red Line by 11.00 am. The Canadian 4th Division passing through the 3rd Division was timed to start its advance to the Blue Line at 12.05 pm. The British Official History commented on the scene, so different from the popular image of the Western Front generated by the photographs of the Somme, Passchendaele and most of what had gone before over the preceding three years of the war:

By this time the mist had cleared and the whole Santerre plateau seen from the air was dotted with parties of infantry, field artillery, cavalry and tanks moving forward. Staff officers were galloping about, many riding horses in battle for the first time, prisoners in formed companies marching back with hardly more escort than the Canadian wounded whom they were carrying, whilst overhead the planes of the Royal Air Force were flying noisily to work.

The heavy artillery had stopped firing, because the infantry they were supporting had advanced beyond their range. Currie was in the process of moving with some of his staff to his advanced headquarters at Gentelles. The Canadian Cavalry Brigade made contact with Brutinel's

---

Left: *German guns captured during the Battle of Amiens. Those in the foreground were taken by the 2nd Canadian Division.*

Independent Force on the Amiens–Roye road. A war of movement had dawned at long last.

Before the mist cleared there had been some fierce engagements. For example the 13th Battalion (Highlanders of Canada) met strong resistance soon after crossing the start line in Hangard Wood. The leading companies bypassed it, leaving the rear companies to deal with it assisted by two tanks. Germans on the far side of the wood were dealt with by two mortars. The Canadians had a harder time in Pelican Ravine (situated

Below: *An armoured car of Brutinel's Independent Force covering the flank of the Canadian Corps on the Amiens–Roye road. The cars were built by the US Autocar Company and armed with two Vickers machine guns.*

Above: *Lancers of the 2nd Cavalry Division en route to Le Quesnel.*

between Hangard Wood and the River Luce) where the German gun lines were stoutly defended by the gunners. To the right the 16th Battalion (Canadian Scottish) advanced with their pipers playing. Their commanding officer remarked that the pipers were very useful, not only to inspire the soldiers, but particularly in the poor visibility to maintain contact between companies. At one stage, the commanding officer and his command group was fired on by a machine gun, killing his piper. The Battalion Scout Officer crept forward along a sunken road and despatched the complete machine gun crew of five with his revolver. He was awarded a bar to his Military Cross. There were many other similar incidents of individual and small group initiative and outstanding soldiering by the Canadians throughout the battle.

At the end of the day's fighting all the objectives in the Canadian sector were in their hands, except on their right. Here, Currie aimed to complete his task by an early morning attack on Le Quesnel. Late in the evening the French took Fresnoy, thus eliminating the danger of a German counterattack on the Canadian right flank from the village. The Canadians had taken over 5,000 prisoners and 161 guns, while suffering about 3,500 casualties themselves. The total German casualties dead, wounded and missing were not known at this stage. What was absolutely clear, in the words of the German official monograph on the battle, summing up the situation: "as the sun set on August 8th on the battlefield the greatest defeat which the German Army had suffered since the beginning of the war was an accomplished fact." Ludendorff wrote; "August 8th was the black day of the German Army in the history of the war … I had no hope of finding a strategic expedient whereby to turn the situation to our advantage."

BATTLE OF AMIENS: 9 TO 11 AUGUST

THE BRITISH OFFICIAL HISTORY COMMENTS ON THE SECOND DAY OF THE BATTLE OF AMIENS, 9 AUGUST 1918, THAT IT WAS "A DAY OF LOST OPPORTUNITIES ALTHOUGH IT BEGAN WELL".

Five miles had been gained on the first day of the battle. The end of the second day saw a three mile advance in the Canadian Corps sector and half that by the Australian Corps. An advance like that in any battle in the preceding three years would have been hailed as a major achievement. But now expectations were much higher.

The event that prompted the "it began well" remark was the capture of Le Quesnel in an early morning attack by two battalions of the 11th Canadian Brigade assisted by Brutinel's Independent Force. But as the Australian historians General John Coates and Peter Dennis comment: "In a process that by now had become habitual on the Western Front, one day's success was almost never followed by equal successes on the next and subsequent days." An advance totalling eight miles by the end of 9 August had resulted in the heavy artillery, vital for counter-battery tasks, being left behind, out of range. Field artillery could catch up, but the heavy guns and their ammunition took days to move forward and get into action. Other logistics problems came to the fore: ammunition of all natures, food, water, fuel for vehicles, fodder for animals, spares and the myriad items that constitute the "lifeblood" of war, had to be taken forward

of the line of communication that now ended eight miles short of where the "customers" – the troops – were. The location of some of the "customers" was still not clear. The extensive trench warfare telephone system had been left behind. New lines were being laid, but this took time, and where they were available it was forbidden to pass operational messages over them for fear of enemy intercept. All this would have been so much easier with portable radios; there were none in 1918.

That second day saw some hard fighting on the Australian left flank, where the British III Corps had failed to secure the ground on the other side of the River Somme. One Australian history is remarkably restrained in its comment, considering the losses suffered by the Australians, because of III Corps failure to keep pace with the Australian advance, attributing this to the difficult ground north of the river: a series of "spines and peninsulas at right-angles to the advance"; and the fact that two of the British divisions in III Corps had been badly mauled in the March fighting. Fortunately, although the Fourth Army was disorganized, the Germans were in a far worse state. They had no well-prepared fallback positions, and much of the artillery belonging to the reinforcement

Left: *King George V knights Lieutenant General John Monash at the Australian Corps at his Corps HQ.*

formations rushing up to stem the flood was left behind in the haste.

The Battle of Amiens was the largest tank battle in the First World War. But another reason for the Fourth Army making only limited gains on the second and subsequent days of the battle was because of the large numbers of losses from mechanical wear and crew-fatigue. Tanks could not operate alone and, when bereft of infantry support, were vulnerable to well-sited field artillery firing over open sights i.e., aiming directly at the tank. No tank in this war, and indeed many in the next, could withstand a direct hit by even a field artillery high explosive shell, still less one from a heavier gun. Some tanks caught fire – "brewed up", in soldiers' argot in the Second World War. Anyone who did not abandon the tank quickly was usually burnt alive.

The RAF had, among its other roles, been tasked with destroying bridges across the River Somme to prevent the arrival of German reserves and to trap their Second Army on the western side of the river. Over 700 missions were flown and 57 tons of bombs dropped. Neither the bombing techniques of the time nor the size of bombs available were up to the task, and no bridges were cut. Bridges are notoriously difficult to cut by aerial bombing, and only relatively recently, about 70 years after the events being described, with the advent of laser guided bombs, can success be more or less guaranteed.

By 10 August, the Fourth Army's attacks were weakening, as the effect noted by John Coates and Peter Dennis became more apparent. The three-mile advance on the 9th, added to the five miles on the day before, merely increased the communication and logistics problem. But despite this, the Canadians, living up to their elite reputation, did best, and advanced two miles. The French on the right flank were equally successful.

Right: *Royal Artillery signallers in a German trench on Chipilly Ridge after its capture by 58th (London) Division on 9 August, the second day of the Battle of Amiens.*

For a while on 11 August, with little gains made, it looked as if Rawlinson would repeat the errors of the past and keep pressing with attacks that would fail. Instead he recommended that the British Third Army, to his north, should now do the attacking. At first Foch tried to persuade Haig – he could only persuade not order – to continue the offensive with the Fourth Army. Rawlinson and Currie persuaded Haig to see sense and attack in a different sector. He agreed, perhaps because he was influenced by them, but also because – contrary to popular perception – he was not stupid. In doing so, he hit upon the winning formula: knowing when to stop attacking in one place and hit somewhere else as quickly as possible, while the enemy's attention and resources were still engaged in the area of the first attack.

The Battle of Amiens ended on 11 August. The British had advanced about 12 miles. More important than ground gained was the damage inflicted on the enemy army. The Germans lost between 48,000 and 75,000 casualties, including 18,350 taken prisoner by the British and 11,373 by the French. British losses were 22,000 dead, wounded and missing, and the French some 24,000.

On 11 August, General Ludendorff told the Kaiser, "Everything I had feared and of which I had so often given warning, had here, in one place, become a reality." After spelling out the reasons, as he saw it, he finished by saying: "The war must be ended."

Meanwhile Haig was about to launch an attack by his Third Army.

Left: *Field Marshal Sir Douglas Haig (left) leading the column, congratulates the Canadian 85th Battalion (Nova Scotia Highlanders).*

19

BATTLE OF ST MIHIEL

GERMAN HOPES THAT THE AMERICAN ARMY WOULD NEVER ARRIVE IN FRANCE IN SUFFICIENT STRENGTH TO HAVE AN EFFECT ON THE OUTCOME OF THE WAR WERE DASHED.

A combination of British and American ships, augmented by German vessels impounded in American harbours when America declared war, transported US troops in ever-larger numbers (over 51 per cent of American soldiers were carried in British merchant ships). A summary of the build up is shown in the green box below. The American 1st Division (the Big Red One) consisting of regular US units, was the first to arrive, on 28 June 1917, although it was not yet ready for operations.

By late summer 1918, the American Expeditionary Force (AEF) had developed from 14,000 (out of a US Army of 25,000) to becoming an operational army in a major war. To put this in perspective, in August 1914 the British Army – ten times bigger at about 250,000 – had been considered tiny by continental European standards. There were differences in the organization of the formations in the AEF from their allies or their enemies. American divisions numbered 27,120 men, over twice the size of their British, French or German equivalents. This was because General Pershing wanted divisions with substantial firepower and an ability to absorb heavy casualties without losing combat power. But American divisions proved to be cumbersome. The span of command was testing for inexperienced major generals, few of whom had previously commanded anything larger than a company in battle, if that. The American soldiers (nicknamed "doughboys") were fit, enthusiastic, and

learned fast. As with most soldiers experiencing combat for the first time, they soon grasped that firepower, thorough training and good tactics win battles; and that propaganda, including belief in racial superiority, are inadequate substitutes for these soldierly skills.

For some weeks, Pershing had planned an attack by the American First Army on the St Mihiel salient, a 32-mile wide bulge, named after the village at its apex. Foch, however, told him to contribute 12 to 16 American divisions to a French attack in the Argonne. Pershing replied; "I decline absolutely to agree to your plan. While our army will fight wherever you decide,

BUILD UP OF AMERICAN TROOPS IN FRANCE

DATE	STRENGTH OF AEF
30 June 1917	14,359
31 December 1917	174,884
31 March 1918	318,621
31 July 1918	1,169,062
31 October 1918	1,867,623

STRENGTH OF BEF IN EUROPE ON 31 OCTOBER 1918

Western Front	1,859,246
Italy	84,000

Left: *American troops attacking at St Mihiel.*

Left: *King George V
(centre, with stick) with
General Pershing inspecting
American troops.*

THE AMERICAN ATTACK,
12 SEPTEMBER 1918

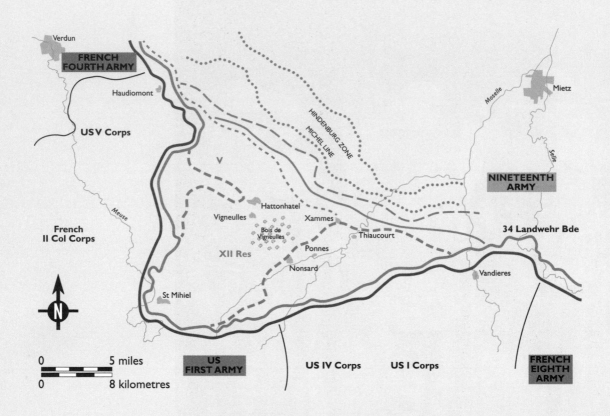

Verdun

FRENCH FOURTH ARMY

Haudiomont

US V Corps

HINDENBURG ZONE

MICHEL LINE

Moselle

Mietz

Seille

NINETEENTH ARMY

V

Meuse

French II Col Corps

Hattonhatel

Vigneulles

Xammes

Bois de Vigneulles

Thiaucourt

34 Landwehr Bde

XII Res

Ponnes

Nonsard

St Mihiel

Vandieres

N

US FIRST ARMY

US IV Corps

US I Corps

FRENCH EIGHTH ARMY

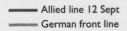

0   5 miles

0   8 kilometres

——— Allied line 12 Sept

——— German front line

– – – German line 12 Sept, pm

· · · · German line 14 Sept, pm

——— German line 16 Sept, pm

– – – German line 18 Sept, pm

Above: *A Renault tank ditched in the region of St Mihiel.*

it will not fight except as an independent American army." Pershing got his way.

At 1.00 am on 12 September 1918, the artillery barrage began, and at 5.00 am it lifted as the leading troops began the assault. For soldiers seeing such a display for the first time, it made a deep impression. A second lieutenant with the 165th Infantry Regiment remembered: "It seemed as if all the artillery in France had suddenly opened up ... the sky was red with big flashes ... the heavier shells made the ground tremble." The American 2nd Division, commanded by a US Marine, Major General John Lejeune, an officer with much experience in combat, included the 4th Marine Brigade in its order of battle. A Marine private in the 5th Marine Regiment wrote: "No Fourth of July display ever equalled this deadly display ... As we passed over

the German lines, I wondered how anyone could live through such a bombardment ... the shell holes were so numerous that we had to walk carefully in order to keep from falling into them."

In the 2nd Division sector, the attack was headed by the 3rd Infantry Brigade, which captured all its objectives, taking some 3,000 prisoners and 120 guns. The 4th Marine Brigade passed through and eventually found itself butting up against the German outposts of the Hindenburg Line. One of the 6th Marines recounted: "These were strong fortifications built of concrete with walls about two feet thick ... they were five feet underground ... well camouflaged ... We also came across many large dugouts, some of them 50 feet underground ..."

The 5th Marines had a fairly easy time reaching

their objectives, followed by digging in to fend off the expected German counter-attacks. The 2nd Battalion, 6th Marines, had a harder fight, and after taking their objective fought off four successive German counter-attacks. However, according to *Soldiers of the Sea: The United States Marine Corps, 1775–1962* by Robert Debs Heinl Jr: "Compared to Belleau Wood and Soissons, St Mihiel was an easy fight for the Marine Brigade." This held good for the whole of the American First Army. The reason for this soon became apparent: the Germans were making preparations for a withdrawal, and most of the positions were held by rear guards. It was, nevertheless, a very valuable experience for the American First Army –

fighting its first battle as a formation – not least for the commanders and staffs (at all levels). They had to plan and orchestrate the articulation of the mass of troops, artillery, tanks, supply trains and medical units that make up an army. Furthermore, as one author remarked: "And, of course, the success improved American morale: already no shrinking violets they now considered themselves ready for anything." He goes on to quote a second lieutenant of the 42nd Division, AEF: "The Boche may not have had much respect for the American Army a few months ago, but from what prisoners say now, we are about as welcome as the proverbial skunk at a lawn party."

Below: *A battery of American artillery near St Mihiel.*

Right: *American gun crew fires a French 75-mm gun at St Mihiel. No guns of American manufacture were in France.*

Left: *Some of the German prisoners taken at St Mihiel.*

PART 6
OTHER FRONTS

THE MIDDLE EAST – THE BATTLE OF MEGIDDO

THE BATTLE OF MEGIDDO WAS AN OUTSTANDING EXAMPLE OF MOBILE WARFARE AND SURPRISE USING MOUNTED TROOPS. IT BEGAN AT 4.30 AM ON 19 SEPTEMBER 1918.

In four hours Lieutenant General Edward Bulfin's infantry had broken through the Turkish defences between the railway line and the sea, and Lieutenant General Henry Chauvel's mounted force was through the gap, his immediate objective of the Plain of Esdraelon (the Armageddon of the Old Testament) north of Megiddo was quickly achieved; as were the crossings over the Jordan by the 4th Cavalry Division. Much of

---

Previous page: A soldier from a Lowland Scots regiment on guard in Salonika harbour.

Left: Soldiers of the 113th (Jat) Regiment firing grenades from a rifle launcher in Mesopotamia.

Below: Turkish prisoners after the Battle of Megiddo. In the foreground are the officers and the Commander of the Turkish 16th Division.

BATTLE OF MEGIDDO (INCLUDING PRELUDE), 16–23 SEPTEMBER 1918

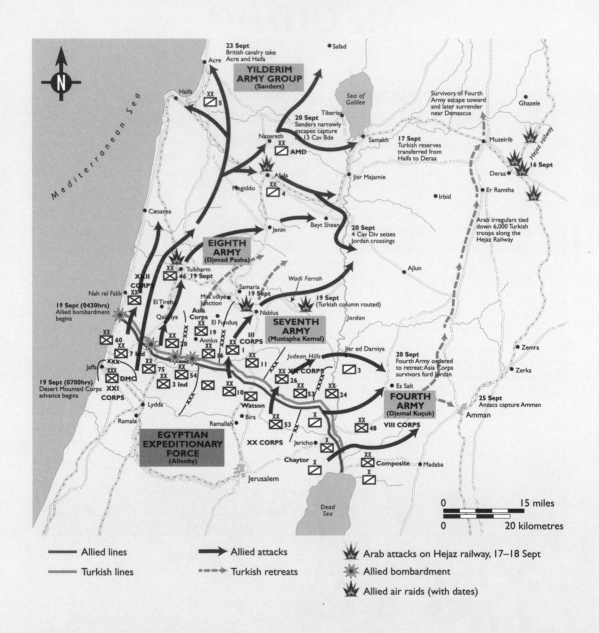

23 Sept British cavalry take Acre and Haifa

YILDERIM ARMY GROUP (Sanders)

20 Sept Sanders narrowly escapes capture by 13 Cav Bde

Survivors of Fourth Army escape toward and later surrender near Damascus

17 Sept Turkish reserves transferred from Haifa to Deraa

Mediterranean Sea

Sea of Galilee

Safad

Acre

Haifa

Tiberias

Samakh

Ghazele

Muzeirib

Nazereth

AMD

Megiddo

Afula

4

Jisr Majamie

Deraa

Er Ramtha

16 Sept

Hejaz railway

Cæsarea

Jenin

Beyt Shean

20 Sept 4 Cav Div seizes Jordan crossings

Irbid

Ajlun

Arab irregulars tied down 6,000 Turkish troops along the Hejaz Railway

EIGHTH ARMY (Djevad Pasha)

Nah rel Falik

Tulkharm

46 **19 Sept**

Samaria **19 Sept**

Wadi Farrah

19 Sept (Turkish column routed)

XXII CORPS

El Tireh

Qalqilya

Mas'udiye Junction

Asia Corps

El Funduq

Nablus

Jordan

Ajlun

Zemra

19 Sept (0430hrs) Allied bombardment begins

60

7 Ind

Annius

SEVENTH ARMY (Mustapha Kemal)

20 Sept Fourth Army ordered to retreat; Asia Corps survivors ford Jordan

Zerka

Jaffa

DMC

75

54

3 Ind

20

III CORPS

Judean Hills

Jisr ed Darniya

3

Es Salt

25 Sept Anzacs capture Amman

19 Sept (0700hrs) Desert Mounted Corps advance begins

XXI CORPS

10

Watson

11

26

XX CORPS

53

24

FOURTH ARMY (Djemal Kuçuk)

Amman

Lydda

Ramala

Ramallah

Bira

53

Judea

VIII CORPS

48

EGYPTIAN EXPEDITIONARY FORCE (Allenby)

XX CORPS

Jericho

Chaytor

Composite

Madaba

Jerusalem

Dead Sea

| 0 | | | 15 miles |
| 0 | | | 20 kilometres |

———	Allied lines	→	Allied attacks	✹	Arab attacks on Hejaz railway, 17–18 Sept
———	Turkish lines	⇢	Turkish retreats	✦	Allied bombardment
				✹	Allied air raids (with dates)

Above: *A group of Australian Light Horsemen of the Australian Mounted Division outside Damascus.*

the success was due to aircraft bombing of key telephone exchanges and the Turkish army wireless station. Fifteen thousand Turkish prisoners were taken, and those enemy who escaped retreated towards Damascus.

PALESTINE

The news of Edmund Allenby's capture of Jerusalem provided a high note on which to end 1917, a year which on the whole had brought little comfort to the Allies. But Allenby's scope for further operations in Palestine was severely limited by the need to send units to France to help stem the German offensives, starting with Operation Michael in March 1918. Not until September did reinforcements from India and Mesopotamia bring the Egyptian Expeditionary Force (EEF) up to sufficient strength for Allenby to continue his advance north.

Allenby set about planning one of the boldest campaigns carried out by the Allies in the whole war. The Turks played into his hands: believing that Russia's collapse would result in Germany wining the war, they sent troops to seize territory in the Caucasus, rather than reinforce their armies in Palestine, which were already outnumbered by the EEF.

Allenby planned to cut the Turkish line of communication, which ran down the Hejaz railway from Damascus to Amman, supplying their Fourth Army. A branch line from Deraa to the west, with extensions running south, fed their Eighth and Seventh Armies. Cuts in the section of line near Deraa would result in the flow of supplies to all Turkish forces drying up. This demolition task Allenby allocated to T. E. Lawrence and the Arabs. He aimed at persuading the Turks that his main attack would be along the

PALESTINE, THE CAMPAIGN

1. After two failed attempts to take Gaza in early 1917, General Murray is replaced by General Allenby

2. Leaving only three divisions at Gaza, General Allenby attacks Beersheba, which falls on 31 October

3. Turkish forces counter-attack but by 7 November are beaten back

4. The Desert Mounted Corps head across country towards the coast, forcing the Turks out of Gaza. British occupy the city 7 November

5. British troops capture Jerusalem on 8 December

6. Colonel T.E. Lawrence and his Arab irregulars disrupt the Hejaz railway

7. Further offensives were curtailed in early 1918 as the Western Front needed reinforcements. It was 19 September before the campaign could resume

8. Allied cavalry capture Nazareth on 20 September

9. By 22 September the Turkish Fourth Army is in retreat. Some units surrender near Damascus, the rest near Amman

British advance → Turkish counter-attack → Turkish front lines
Arab attacks → Turkish retreat

Above: *Indian soldiers engage a Turkish aircraft with a Lewis Gun in Mesopotamia.*

Jordan Valley. He actually intended to attack north along the west coast. Having made a gap between the railway line and the sea, a mass of cavalry would advance north along the coast and swing in behind the Turkish Seventh and Eighth Armies. Allenby moved three cavalry divisions from the Jordan Valley to the coast.

On 16 September, Allenby had 35,000 infantry, 9,000 cavalry and 400 guns poised for his offensive. After overwhelming the Turks with a massive artillery barrage, Allenby's infantry levered open a gap for his cavalry of the Desert Mounted Corps who poured through. The 5th Cavalry Division reached Megiddo on 19 September, and Nazareth fell on 20 September. The German General Otto Liman von Sanders, commander of the Yildirim

Army Group, got out just in time to avoid being taken prisoner. The retreat of the Turkish Eighth and Seventh Armies was turned into a rout by the advance of the EEF XX Corps. Some of Turkish Fourth Army escaped north to Damascus, while the majority were cut off and surrendered outside Amman.

On 1 October the Australians and Arabs were the first of Allenby's EEF to enter Damascus. He had advanced 300 miles, captured 75,000 prisoners, 360 guns and most of the Turkish transport and supplies. It cost Allenby 5,720 casualties: a stunning victory.

Turkey now sought peace and signed an Armistice with the Entente Allies on 30 October 1918.

In Mesopotamia, offensive operations had also closed down in early 1918, and on being renewed resulted

in the British entering Mosul on 2 November 1918, following the signing of the armistice with Turkey on 30 October.

RECKONING

The campaigns in the Middle East did not have the effect on the main theatre of operations, the Western Front, hoped for by the likes of Lloyd George. They merely tied up thousands of troops and massive resources that would have been better employed on the main point of effort. The German armies in the West did not retreat because of the defeat of the Turks in the Middle East, but, as will be related in later chapters, as a result of the efforts of British, French and American armies on the Western Front.

The repercussions of the British campaigns in Palestine and Mesopotamia are with us to this day, 100 years later, in the unhappy events that continue to trouble parts of the Middle East. It would arguably have been better for all concerned, not least the inhabitants of that region, had Britain, and France, contented themselves with considerably less ambitious political and territorial gains in the Middle East.

Left: *Before the Battle of Megiddo, soldiers of 2nd Battalion, The Black Watch, training on the coast near Arsuf, on the Plain of Sharon, between the railway line and the sea, south of where Bulfin's infantry broke through.*

21

THE BALKANS

FOR REASONS THAT ARE TOO CONVOLUTED TO EXPLORE HERE, THE BALKANS ARE POPULARLY DEPICTED AS THE SOURCE OF THE SPARK THAT LIT THE FUSE FOR THE ERUPTION OF THE FIRST WORLD WAR. BUT FOR THE FIRST SIX MONTHS OF THE WAR, FIGHTING IN THE BALKANS WAS CONFINED TO SERBIA VERSUS AUSTRIA-HUNGARY: ALL OTHER POWERS ON BOTH SIDES WERE TOO BUSY ELSEWHERE.

Early in 1915, the Serbs asked for help from their Entente Allies, and the French and British proposed sending a joint force to Salonika, which, despite being in Greece, was the only port not in Austrian hands within range of the Serbian front. The plan came to naught because King Constantine of Greece vetoed the proposal. Allied failure at Gallipoli persuaded Bulgaria to join the German side. That, and the need to keep the land supply routes open to their Turkish allies, galvanized Germany into joining Austrian operations against

Left: *French General Maurice Sarrail inspecting Russian troops on their arrival at Salonika on 30 July 1916. By 1918 Russian troops had been withdrawn.*

Above: *British troops constructing a shell-proof field gun position as part of the 'birdcage' defence line in the hills north of Salonika, March 1916.*

Above: Macedonian terrain in the area of Lake Doiran where the British diversionary assault took place as part of the Allied advance.

the Serbs. Until then, the Austrians had been notably unsuccessful against the Serb Army. This was paradoxical bearing in mind that the Austrian yearning to seek any excuse to crush Serbia had been a contributory cause of the war in the first place.

Greece had treaty obligations to Serbia requiring the commitment of troops in the event of a Bulgarian attack – but only if the Allies could produce an equal force. In response to Bulgaria's decision to support Germany and Austria, the French General Maurice Sarrail was ordered to Salonika with four divisions in September 1915. The Austro-German attack began the next day, and by mid-November the Serbian Army had been driven into Albania. Sarrail, having advanced some way into Serbia was soon stopped, and he withdrew to Salonika. Here he was joined by British troops after the evacuation of Gallipoli.

As time passed, what became known as the Allied Armies of the Orient were joined by a revitalized Serbian Army, as well as Italians, Russians and Romanians, and eventually Greeks, after the Allies had deposed King Constantine in June 1917. The Commander-in-Chief of the German Army, General Erich von Falkenhayn, abandoned plans for a large-scale offensive in the Balkans, because he needed as many troops as possible for his 1916 assault on Verdun. Thereafter Germany continued with a policy of avoiding an attack on Salonika on the grounds that large numbers of Allied troops were languishing in what the Germans called "Germany's biggest internment camp", and consequently were not available for operations elsewhere. At its peak the Allied Army comprised some 600,000 men, facing about 450,000 Bulgarians, who relied on the difficulties of campaigning in the demanding terrain to pin down their

GENERAL LOUIS FRANCHET D'ESPÈREY – "DESPERATE FRANKIE"

A man of great energy, and of intimidating aspect, d'Espèrey was sometimes known as "Desperate Frankie" by his British allies, for his sometimes risk-taking propensity. On the outbreak of the war, he commanded I Corps, part of General Charles Lanrezac's French Fifth Army on the left of the French line. He eventually relieved Lanrezac, who was sacked for lack of offensive spirit. He commanded the Fifth Army at the first Battle of the Marne where his efforts were rewarded by promotion to command the Eastern Army Group. When General Joseph Joffre was removed as Commander-in-Chief, d'Espèrey was considered as his replacement. But his steadfast Roman Catholicism was a severe disadvantage in the opinion of the powerful anti-clericalism of many French senior officers and politicians. The job went to Robert Nivelle, a decision that was to prove dire. D'Espèrey was given command of the Army Group in Champagne, where his refusal to deploy in depth during the German offensives in early 1918 led to much ground in his sector being lost in May. He was rightly held responsible and sent off to the backwater of Salonika. Here he breathed life into the campaign and gained a series of stunning successes.

Above: *Lightly injured or sick Highland soldiers from British 77th Brigade being carried to a dressing station by mule-borne cacholet.*

Right: *A Serb mountain battery moving through a Macedonian village. These small howitzers could be broken down to be loaded onto mules, and quickly re-assembled for action.*

more numerous opponent. Apart from a few sporadic local actions, Allied troops remained in Salonika, doing very little until September 1918. One activity seems to have been gardening, hence the derogatory nickname for the force, "the gardeners of Salonika".

BREAKOUT

In June 1918, the fearsome and energetic General d'Espèrey took command of the Allied Armies of the Orient at Salonika. Taking advantage of the withdrawal of most German troops to the Western Front, d'Espèrey mounted an attack on the Bulgarians on 15 September. Although he was outnumbered, his force of Serbs, Czechs, Italians, French and British inflicted a major defeat on the Bulgarians. By the night of 17 September the Serbs had advanced 20 miles. Soon the Bulgarians were in full retreat. At Kosturino, British aircraft bombed the Bulgarians, turning the retreat into a rout,

splitting open the front. On 26 September British troops reached Strumitsa, and on the 29th, French cavalry seized Skopje on the Macedonian/Serbian border. Bulgaria sued for peace and was granted a ceasefire. But d'Espèrey kept advancing. He crossed the Danube on 10 November, determined to head for Budapest and Dresden, only halting his advance when on 11 November Germany's acceptance of an Armistice ended hostilities.

It is generally accepted that the campaign was largely irrelevant to the outcome of the war, until the last few weeks. Although Ludendorff, possibly casting around for any excuse to explain his failure to win, deemed it to have been a decisive factor in Germany's defeat. Allied troops suffered around 20,000 battle casualties during the whole campaign, but sickness took a far greater toll: nearly 450,000 were invalided out of the theatre with malaria alone by late 1918.

Below: *Highlanders of the British Army somewhere in Macedonia, or "Muckydonia" to them. Place and date unknown.*

22

ITALY, THE BATTLE OF VITTORIO VENETO

FOLLOWING THE ITALIAN DEFEAT OF THE AUSTRIANS ON THE PIAVE IN JUNE, GENERAL ARMANDO DIAZ, THE ITALIAN ARMY CHIEF OF STAFF, WAS HESITANT ABOUT MOUNTING AN OFFENSIVE. HE LACKED RESERVES AND THE AUSTRIANS OUTNUMBERED THE ITALIAN ARMY.

In the autumn of 1918, with German troops on the Western Front fully engaged with a series of Allied attacks, Foch pressed Diaz to mount an offensive. By now Diaz had been reinforced by British, French and American formations. To begin with even this was insufficient to persuade him to attack, until the political scene changed drastically. On 26 September, Bulgaria sued for peace. This was followed on 4 October by Austria and Germany indicating a willingness to accept President Woodrow Wilson's Fourteen Points and requesting an armistice, which at that time was not accepted. Italy needed to be seen to be winning and pushing the Austrians back in order to be in the strongest possible bargaining position when the time came for peace terms to be hammered out. Italy had switched sides in 1915 in exchange for Entente promises that Tyrol, Trieste, Gorizia, Istria and northern Dalmatia would be stripped from the Austro-Hungarian Empire and handed over to Italy. If the Italians did not stir themselves into action, the Entente Allies might be less inclined to support their claim to these slices of Austro-Hungarian soil. Accordingly, Diaz decided to attack.

The Italians planned a two-pronged offensive. The Italian Eighth, Tenth and Twelfth Armies, with British and French divisions, would attack on the Piave river, aiming to advance and secure Vittorio Veneto. At the same time, the Italian Fourth Army was to attack Monte Grappa, a key piece of terrain on the Twelfth Army's left flank, where the Piave turns 90 degrees and debouches onto the plains north of Venice. Although the fighting qualities of the Austrians had definitely deteriorated, and morale was low, their commanders were well aware that the more Italian territory they retained if and when there was an Armistice the greater chance they would have of

Above: *Italian officers inspect an Austro-Hungarian dug-out on the Val d'Assa mountain road.*

retaining some of their territory coveted by the Italians. It
was therefore in Austria's interests to fight hard.

Operations began on 23 October with the Fourth
Army's attack on Monte Grappa. The Austrians
defended resolutely, halting the Italians. The following
day, the Austrian Sixth Army fought the Italian Eighth
Army to a standstill. But on each side of the Italian
Eighth Army the situation was much more encouraging.
French formations under the Italian Twelfth Army
seized a foothold across the Piave, while two British
divisions, under the Earl of Cavan, attached to the
Italian Tenth Army, secured a sizeable bridgehead two
miles deep and four miles wide on the right and built
bridges. Cavan's action was the key to the success of
the operation. At the start of the offensive, Italian
engineers had attempted to bridge the Piave in 11
places. Floodwater had destroyed most of the bridges
in the Eighth and Twelfth Army sectors. So the Eighth
Army Commander pushed one of his corps across the
British bridges, with orders to swing left, once across,
and establish a foothold across the Piave on the Eighth
Army's front. Once this was achieved the bridgehead

for the three attacking armies was extended to 10 miles
wide and four miles deep. A wedge had been driven
between the Austrian Fifth and Sixth Armies, and
33,000 prisoners were taken.

An Italian formation took Vittorio Veneto on
30 October, and Austrian resistance began to crumble.
Belluno fell on 1 November, and the River Tagliamento
was crossed on 2 November. On the left flank of the
Italian front, British and French formations under the
Italian Sixth Army took the key rail junction of Trento
on 3 November. That same day an Allied naval force
captured the Austrian port of Trieste at the head of the
Gulf of Venice, one of Italy's key objectives.

As the Austrian front split apart in several places, the
Austro-Hungarian Army retreat turned into headlong
flight. On 30 October Austria asked for an armistice.
This was granted on 3 November, and hostilities in the
Italian theatre ended on the 4th. Allied casualties for the
Battle of Vittorio Veneto totalled over 35,000, far lower
than the Austro-Hungarian toll, which included over
half a million prisoners. In Italian eyes, their humiliating
defeat at Caporetto had been avenged.

Below: *Soldiers of the 2nd Battalion, The Gordon Highlanders, escorting Austro-Hungarian prisoners over a bridge across the River Piave, November 1918.*

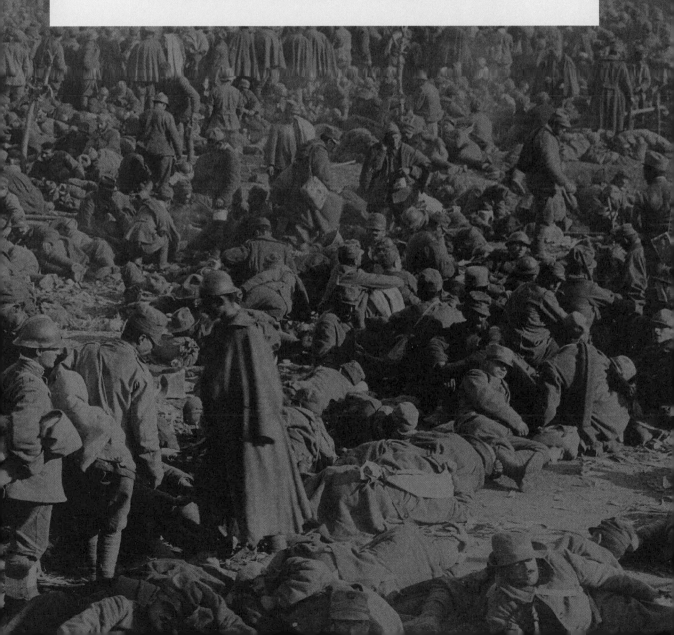

PART 7
CONTINUING THE ADVANCE ON THE WESTERN FRONT

BATTLES OF ALBERT/SCARPE

THE NEXT MAJOR OFFENSIVE AFTER THE BATTLE OF AMIENS TOOK PLACE ON 21 AUGUST, BY GENERAL SIR JULIAN BYNG'S THIRD ARMY. BETWEEN THEN AND EARLY SEPTEMBER THE BEF LAUNCHED A SERIES OF ATTACKS BY FOURTH ARMY AND FIRST ARMY.

The series of blows inflicted on the Germans served to unbalance them as they attempted to move reserves to meet each attack. The BEF was able to mount a "ripple" of blows at different places along its front because there was plenty of artillery. Hence there was no need for long pauses between each "punch" to allow guns and ammunition to be moved to positions to support the attacks. Despite its recent attack at Amiens, the Fourth Army still had the most guns (1,736); the Third Army had 1,294, Second Army 1,218, and the First Army 1,216. This quantity of artillery, a total of 5,464 guns, was over 17 times the number of guns in the BEF at the Battle of Mons in 1914.

Haig met Byng on 19 August and, according to Haig's diary, told him, "Now is the time to act with boldness … if only we hit the enemy hard enough, and continue to press him, that he will give way …" Byng's offensive, the Battle of Albert, saw the BEF cross the old Somme battlefield of 1916 in a few days.

On 23 August Rawlinson's Fourth Army attacked on Third Army's right. Haig noted in his diary that he issued a note to all his Army Commanders ordering them to pass to all units under their command, "It is no longer necessary to advance step by step in regular lines as in

the 1916–17 battles. All units must go straight for their objectives, while reserves should be pushed in where we are gaining ground … risks which a month ago would have been criminal to incur, ought now to be incurred as a duty."

On 24 August, Haig told General Sir Henry Horne to mount a surprise attack with his First Army astride the Cambrai road. Horne's attack, the Battle of the Scarpe, began on 26 August and made good progress. These successive blows drove the Germans back and on 3 September they began their withdrawal to the Hindenburg Line. Arguably the two most remarkable efforts among a string of stunning successes were the battles fought by Monash's Australian Corps as part of Fourth Army, and Currie's Canadian Corps in First Army.

Rawlinson wanted the Fourth Army to take Péronne "on the run", which was very ambitious, as flooded marshes stood between the Fourth Army and the town. He gave the task to the Australian Corps. As part of the plan, Monash had to take Mont St Quentin, which was just to the north of Péronne, and garrisoned by the 2nd Prussian Guards Division. Monash's first attempt was unsuccessful. So he formed a new plan, which involved crossing the River Somme in the north, instead

---

Left: Battle of the Scarpe, after the capture of Greenland Hill by the 51st (Highland) Division, a patrol of the 6th Battalion Seaforth Highlanders clearing a dugout; very likely a posed photograph. Highlanders wore the kilt, with a khaki apron over it.

Previous page: Masses of Italian prisoners held outdoors in Vittorio, November 1917.

THE BRITISH ADVANCE, AUGUST–SEPTEMBER

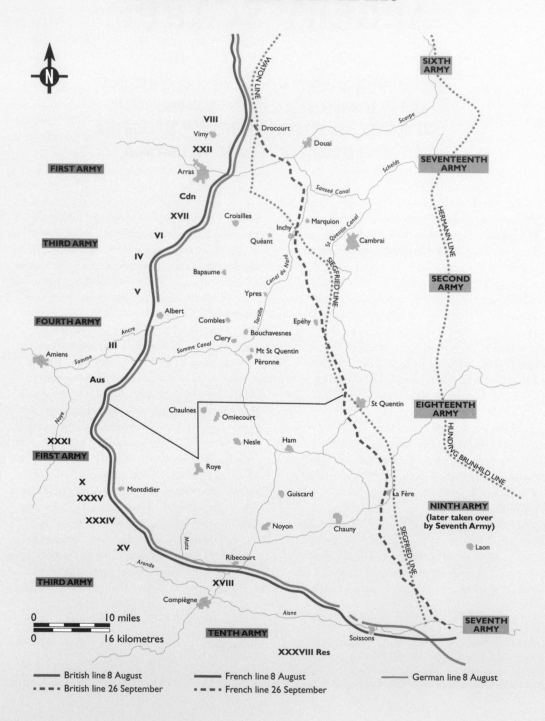

N

VIII
Vimy
XXII
Arras
Cdn
XVII
VI
IV
V
Albert
III
Amiens
Aus
XXXI
X
XXXV
XXXIV
XV
XVIII
Compiègne

FIRST ARMY

THIRD ARMY

FOURTH ARMY

FIRST ARMY

THIRD ARMY

TENTH ARMY

XXXVIII Res

Drocourt
Douai
Croisilles
Inchy
Quéant
Marquion
Cambrai
Bapaume
Ypres
Combles
Clery
Bouchavesnes
Epéhy
Mt St Quentin
Pèronne
Chaulnes
Omiecourt
Nesle
Ham
Roye
Montdidier
Guiscard
Noyon
Chauny
La Fère
Laon
Ribecourt
Soissons

SIXTH ARMY
SEVENTEENTH ARMY
SECOND ARMY
EIGHTEENTH ARMY
NINTH ARMY
(later taken over by Seventh Army)
SEVENTH ARMY

WOTON LINE
Scarpe
Scheldt
Sanseé Canal
St Quentin Canal
HERMANN LINE
Canal du Nord
SIEGFRIED LINE
Tortille
Somme Canal
Ancre
Somme
Noye
Matz
Aronde
Aisne
HUNDING BRUNHILD LINE
SIEGFRIED LINE
St Quentin

0 ———— 10 miles
0 ———— 16 kilometres

—— British line 8 August   —— French line 8 August   —— German line 8 August
- - - British line 26 September   - - - French line 26 September

of attacking frontally from the west. The battle lasted continuously for four days. But the many setbacks were overcome thanks to the self-reliant Australian soldiers, who despite being desperately tired, and whose battalions and companies were understrength, performed a feat of arms that few other troops could have matched. By 4 September all objectives had been taken.

Meanwhile, in First Army, Lieutenant General Sir Arthur Currie's Canadian Corps was to capture the Drocourt–Quéant position. It consisted of a forward defence system of two lines of trenches, on a forward slope, and further back, on a reverse slope, a support defence system of two lines of trenches. It lacked the depth of the Hindenburg Line, but the D..ing. Switch connecting it with the Hindenburg position acted as a third line of defences. Starting at 5.00 am on 2 September, the Canadians got through the forward defence system quite quickly and pushed on past the support system to capture the village of Dury. Here they consolidated, ready

to receive the usual German counter-attack. When it came, some ground was lost, but then quickly regained in some fierce fighting, including a bayonet charge.

Further south, the 16th Battalion of the 1st Canadian Division were pinned down by machine guns and thick belts of uncut wire. At that moment a British tank joined them, and Lance Corporal William Metcalf jumped up and waved a signal flag that directed to the enemy. On capturing the trench on the other side of the wire, the Canadians found that 17 enemy machine guns had been causing the trouble. As the Canadians penetrated deeper into the position, the enemy began surrendering in large numbers. The next day, the Germans in this sector began their withdrawal to the Hindenburg Line.

The Germans finished retreating and consolidated along the Hindenburg Line on 11 September. Except for Armentières and the Messines Ridge, they relinquished all the ground taken in March and April. The BEF followed up, relaying railway lines and preparing the lines of communication in order to allow Haig to fulfil his aim of smashing through the Hindenburg Line before winter set in.

_____

Below: *Shaving in a shell hole, or the remnants of a dugout hit by a large shell.*

Below: *Ruins of Monchy-le-Preux, captured by the 2nd and 3rd Canadian Divisions.*

24

SITUATION AND PLANS, 26 SEPTEMBER 1918

| 0 | 20 | 40 | 60 | 80 | 100 miles |
| 0 | 30 | 60 | 90 | 120 | 150 kilometres |

British and American Armies — Direction of attacks
French and Belgian Armies — Line on 8 August 1918

Time schedule for general offensive as ordered by General Foch on 23 September 1918
Tout le monde à la bataille — Everybody into battle

1. 26 September   Franco/American attack between the Suippe and the Meuse
2. 27 September   Attack by British First and Third Armies in the general direction of Cambrai
3. 28 September   An attack by the Flanders Group of Armies between the sea and the Lys, under the command of the King of the Belgians
4. 29 September   An attack by the British Fourth Army, supported by the French First Army in the direction of Busigny

MEUSE/ARGONNE – FRENCH AND AMERICANS

IN ACCORDANCE WITH FOCH'S ORDERS THE FRANCO-AMERICAN ATTACK IN THE ARGONNE TOOK PLACE ON 26 SEPTEMBER – A MERE 10 DAYS AFTER THE END OF THE ST MIHIEL OFFENSIVE.

The principal objective for the French and Americans was Mézières, a key junction on the east–west railway line. Similarly, British attacks aimed at Cambrai and St Quentin endangered vital north–south lines. If the Germans lost these lines, or even if they came within long-range artillery fire, the effect on their logistics would be catastrophic. Mézières was 30 miles from the start line for the Franco-American attack, and in between, facing the Americans, was the Argonne Forest. This forest, between two rivers – the Aisne and the Aire – was

Above: *American troops in Montfaucon passing the house used by Crown Prince Wilhelm in 1916 when commanding the German Fifth Army at the Battle of Verdun.*

18681

Above: *Troops of American 39th Infantry in defensive positions.*

Right: *American trucks loaded with troops in a traffic jam in Limey, 13 September 1918. A problem for the movements staff to sort out.*

a natural defensive position, which the Germans had thickened up by four lines of defence. Between the Aire and the Meuse less thickly wooded hill features formed another natural defensive position, of which Montfaucon (1,200 feet) was the highest. Montfaucon dominated the terrain on its flanks, which was bounded by the Aire and the Meuse, and formed two five-mile wide "alleyways" funnelling the American attack.

The Americans were faced with a daunting enough task, made more complicated by having to move some 400,000 troops from the St Mihiel sector before the attack could be launched. These men replaced French divisions, around 220,000 strong, who had to be withdrawn to make space for the incoming formations. Over three-quarters of a million soldiers had to be

redeployed in a few days – nearly twice the pre-war population of Birmingham (525,833). About 418,000 soldiers were transported by truck. The remainder marched, along with more than 90,000 horses and mules. That was not all. The troops, animals and trucks would consume tons of fodder, petrol and rations daily. Nearly 3,000 guns and 40,000 tons of ammunition had also to be moved into position – ammunition expenditure would be about 3,000 tons a day. Colonel George C. Marshall, of the American First Army operations staff, was in overall control of this mass-migration. Truly, those who mock soldiers know nothing of war.

At dawn on 26 September, Pershing's American First Army and Gouraud's French Fourth Army attacked on a 40-mile front. On the first day, the fiercest fighting took

THE AMERICAN-FRENCH ADVANCE, 26 SEPTEMBER–3 OCTOBER 1918

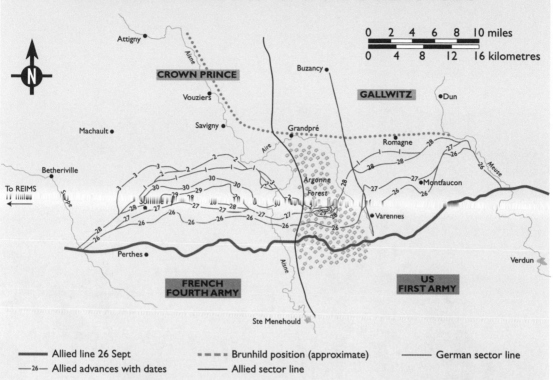

Attigny

CROWN PRINCE

Buzancy

Vouziers

GALLWITZ

Dun

Machault

Savigny

Grandpré

Romagne

Aire

Argonne Forest

Montfaucon

Betheriville

To REIMS

Varennes

Perthes

Verdun

FRENCH
FOURTH ARMY

US
FIRST ARMY

Ste Menehould

0   2   4   6   8   10 miles
0   4   8   12   16 kilometres

———— Allied line 26 Sept
—26— Allied advances with dates
▪ ▪ ▪ ▪ Brunhild position (approximate)
———— Allied sector line
———— German sector line

Below: *An American 340-mm gun, of French manufacture, under camouflage covering near Baleycourt, 26 September 1918.*

Top: *French Renault FT-17 tanks, in American service, moving up to a forward area near Boureville (Forest of Argonne), 26 September 1918.*

Bottom: *An American 340-mm railway gun firing at Baleycourt near Verdun, 26 September 1918.*

COLONEL GEORGE C. MARSHALL

This photograph shows Marshall as a Colonel just after the war. He graduated from the Virginia Military Institute in 1901, and was commissioned as a second lieutenant in the US Army in 1902. Throughout his early military career he showed an exceptional talent for staff work, and consequently was given responsibility beyond his rank. He greatly impressed his superiors, notably General Pershing, who assigned him to his operations staff in France. Marshall played a major role in planning the St Mihiel and Argonne offensives. He had an excellent reputation for working with Allied commands and their headquarters. Before the Second World War President Roosevelt selected him to be Army Chief of Staff (the professional head of the US Army). In that capacity he oversaw the development of the US Army before and during the war. He later became Roosevelt's chief military adviser and a key member of the Joint Chiefs of Staff (American and British) who were responsible for the overall Allied direction of the Second World War on all fronts in which the US and UK took part.

place around Montfaucon. General Hunter Liggett of the American I Corps described the terrain as being worse than the Virginia wilderness in which Lee and Grant had slugged it out in 1864. Between them the French and Americans had nearly 500 tanks, mainly light Renaults. But the wooded terrain was bad tank country, and the Germans had sown anti-tank minefields consisting of 5.9-inch shells buried in the ground.

On 27 September, additional German divisions rushed into the battle, mounting counter-attacks in their usual well-planned and expertly conducted way. The Franco-American advance slowed and eventually stopped on 30 September, having gained about eight miles of ground and around 18,000 prisoners and 200 guns. Foch called a halt to the operation. After the easy success at St Mihiel, this battle was a revelation to the Americans, many in action for the first time. This was also the first time that their senior commanders had handled such large formations in battle. There seems to have been some impatience on the part of Pershing and some of his First Army staff at the slow rate of advance. Co-operation between units was made difficult

by the rough wooded terrain. Infantry and artillery did not work well together: this was hardly surprising as they had not trained together sufficiently, in some cases not at all, and for many this was their first battle.

Pershing was dismissive of French and British tactics, believing them too timid. His ideas were old-fashioned, in some ways harking back to the way the Allies had fought in 1916 and 1917: throwing enthusiastic young soldiers into mass, frontal assaults. Some American formations were of very high quality, notably the joint Army/United States Marine Corps 2nd Division commanded by Major General John Lejeune USMC, and the 42nd (Rainbow) Division commanded by the youthful Major General Douglas MacArthur (both he and Marshall would become household names in the next war). Other divisions at this stage in the war were not in the same league, through no fault of theirs, although the potential was there. Pershing ignored the battle techniques that had evolved by 1918 and his soldiers paid the price. There was much to learn, the Americans would learn fast, and they would soon be attacking again.

PART 8
FINAL BATTLES

CANAL DU NORD AND FLANDERS

ON 27 SEPTEMBER 1918, IT WAS THE TURN OF THE BRITISH FIRST AND THIRD ARMIES TO ATTACK. GENERAL SIR HENRY HORNE'S FIRST ARMY'S TASK WAS TO SECURE THE BOURLON RIDGE AND PROTECT BYNG'S THIRD ARMY AS IT ADVANCED TO SEIZE CROSSINGS OF THE SCHELDT CANAL.

Horne gave Lieutenant General Sir Arthur Currie's Canadians the toughest task: to force the crossing of the Canal du Nord. The unfinished canal was mainly dry, but a formidable obstacle, varying from 30 to 60 feet deep and 90 to 120 feet wide. Some sections were filled with barbed wire. About 300 yards beyond the Canal was the Canal du Nord defence line, and, beyond again, in the southern portion of the Canadian attack sector, the Marquion and Marcoing lines. The Canadians were to cross the canal on a narrow frontage of 2,500 yards, but as they advanced the width of their frontage would expand to 9,500 yards. Currie decided that his 4th and 1st Divisions would lead, with 3rd Canadian and 11th British Divisions coming up on either side as the advance progressed. There was no preliminary bombardment. At 5.20 am a massive creeping barrage rained down from guns, mortars and massed Vickers machine guns. By the end of the day the Canadians had advanced beyond all their objectives for 27 September.

The British Third Army also made good progress. The northern sector of Third Army's front included the Canal du Nord. The task of seizing the crossing was given to the Guards Division – this was a formation with a reputation second to none, and so often given the hardest task to perform, in the knowledge that, like the Australians and Canadians, no effort would be spared to achieve the objective. By 28 September both First and Third Armies had torn a hole 12 miles wide and six deep in the German defences. Neither First nor Third Armies had it all their way, and as the battle went on there was some very heavy fighting. On 29 September the Canadians suffered over 2,000 casualties, and by 1 October the Corps was very weary – not surprising after five days of fighting without pause for breath.

On 28 September the Flanders Group started its offensive. This formation consisted of 12 infantry divisions and a cavalry division of the Belgian Army, supported by six infantry divisions and three cavalry divisions of the French Army, and the British Second Army of 10 divisions. The whole Group was commanded by King Albert of the Belgians. Up to now, except for defensive action in 1914, the Belgian Army had played a very minor part in the war.

The old soldiers of the British Second Army in 1918 had fought in this region before. A tiny handful had participated in the First Battle of Ypres in 1914, when the regular formations of the original BEF had held the German Army at enormous cost in casualties. A few more had fought in the horrific conditions of Third Ypres in 1917 (popularly called Passchendaele, although that was but one of the battles in four months of trial).

Previous page: *Dawn barrage, Canal du Nord, 60-pdr gun firing, with, silhouetted on the skyline, artillery moving forward.*

Left: *Royal Engineers bridging the Canal du Nord near Moeuvres, 28 September 1918.*

Above: *Soldiers of the 16th Infantry Battalion (Canadian Scottish) near Inchy during the Canadian crossing of the Canal du Nord, 27 September 1918.*

Most recently, some had fought there in the Battle of the Lys earlier in 1918. Brigadier General J.L. Jack had first encountered the Ypres salient in 1914 as a captain in the First Battalion the Cameronians, and again as a lieutenant colonel commanding the 2nd West Yorkshires in 1917. Now he was commanding the 28th Brigade. He wrote in his diary, referring to 1917: "the bones of most of my officers and many of my other ranks lie between here and Zonnebeke."

This was different. On 28 September alone the two left-hand corps of Second Army advanced between four and a half and six miles. Brigadier General Jack observed in his diary: "The day's success has been astonishing; an advance of over five miles (more than in four months of bloody

fighting last year) … the good leading and drive from all ranks from sunrise to sundown, through this bullet-swept wilderness, has been admirable, hustling the enemy off his feet." British soldiers who had endured the agony of Third Ypres could hardly believe that places that had taken weeks to capture were secured in two days at most.

On 2 October, the offensive in Flanders was halted to allow some reorganization and resupply. On that day, the RAF made history by dropping rations to the Belgians and French who had consumed all their food. Eighty aircraft dropped 15,000 rations, totalling 13 tons. Thrown out at 300 feet, without benefit of parachute, the soft mud allowed most of the bags that were dropped to remain intact.

FIRST ARMY OPERATIONS OF THE RIGHT WING, 27 SEPTEMBER–7 OCTOBER 1918

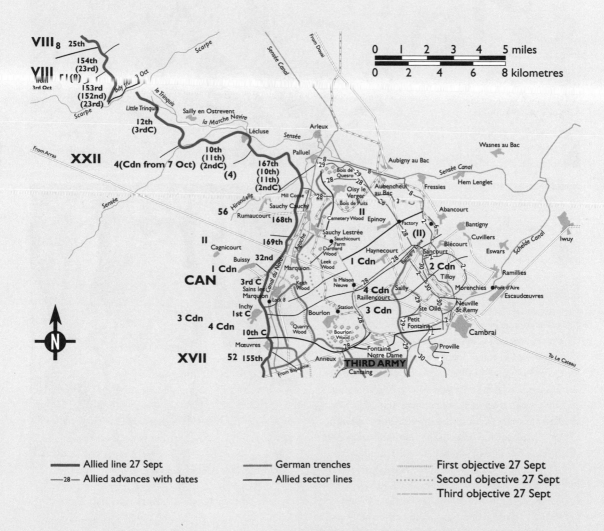

▬▬▬ Allied line 27 Sept	▬▬▬ German trenches	⋯⋯⋯ First objective 27 Sept
—28— Allied advances with dates	▬▬▬ Allied sector lines	·········· Second objective 27 Sept
		— — — Third objective 27 Sept

GENERAL SIR HENRY HORNE

General Sir Henry Horne was the only artillery officer to command a British army in the First World War, and indeed ever. Commissioned into the Royal Artillery in 1880, he participated in the Boer War before serving on the First Corps staff under Lieutenant General Sir Douglas Haig in the two years preceding the First World War. He served with distinction in the first months of the war in France and Flanders, being promoted to command Second Division in time to take part in the Battles of Festubert in May 1915, and Loos in September that year. After a spell in Egypt commanding XV Corps defending the Suez Canal, Horne returned with XV Corps to the Western Front in time to take part in the Battle of the Somme. The New Zealanders of his corps captured Flers in the first tank attack in history. The next year he commanded the First Army in the engagement at Vimy Ridge. Horne's First Army played a full part in the great advance of the "hundred days" following the Battle of Amiens. After the war he was raised to the peerage.

Opposite: *Battle of the Canal du Nord. German prisoners taken near Moeuvres in the 4th Canadian Division's sector during the crossing of the Canal du Nord, 27 September 1918.*

Above: *Canal du Nord infantry reserves going forward, 4th Canadian Division, 27 September 1918.*

26

BREACHING THE HINDENBURG LINE

ON 29 SEPTEMBER, BRITISH FOURTH ARMY ATTACKED THE HINDENBURG LINE, HAVING MADE PRELIMINARY MOVES 11 DAYS EARLIER.

The attack on the Hindenburg Line was made complicated by a number of factors. Of these, the principal ones were: the defence was in great depth, and the main role in the attack was to be carried out by Lieutenant General Sir John Monash's Australian Corps who were weary and understrength.

At 5.20 am on 18 September, the attack on what was designated the outpost line of the Hindenburg Line went in. This line included three old British trench lines, with a further one in depth, the Advance Hindenburg System, or "Ridge Line". The British III Corps attacked in the north; the Australian Corps in the centre, with 4th and 1st Australian Divisions forward, and British IX Corps in the south. By the end of the day, the Australians had overrun the old British defensive lines and German positions on the Ridge Line. In the south and north events had not gone so well. The British IX Corps had been hit by enfilade fire when a planned French attack to their right had fizzled out. In the north British III Corps had been held up by strongly defended villages and a fresh German division whose presence was not known beforehand. Nevertheless, the British artillery had completely dominated their German opponents to the extent that only a few rounds were fired by them. The creeping barrages fired by the British proved so successful that many German defenders offered little resistance

and surrendered to Australian attackers following close up behind them. Where the British formations on the flanks "lost" the supporting barrage, either through inexperience or because of an over-complicated plan involving too many changes of direction, German machine guns caused heavy casualties.

Monash planned the next stage with his customary thoroughness. However, Rawlinson, commanding Fourth Army, ordered that the frontage of the assault be increased to prevent enfilade fire on the attacking troops. The British 46th Division would now cross the St Quentin Canal south of the tunnel (see next chapter). Rawlinson also decided that the US 27th Division was to mount a preliminary operation including taking Quennemont Farm, Gillemont Farm, and the Knoll to advance the line.

In the early morning of 27 September, the US 27th Division's units were heavily engaged by the German 153rd Regiment, and hurled back. The Americans were so disorientated by fog that for days no one could establish what their attack had achieved and consequently whether or not the creeping barrage for the main attack could be used without causing casualties to American troops.

Although the main attack on the Hindenburg Line began at 5.50 am on 29 September, the American 27th Division, with tank support, began to advance an hour early, at 4.50 am. The division tried to rush the first

Left: *Australians attacking the Hindenburg outpost line, 18 September 1918.*

BREAKING THE HINDENBURG LINE,
29 SEPTEMBER 1918

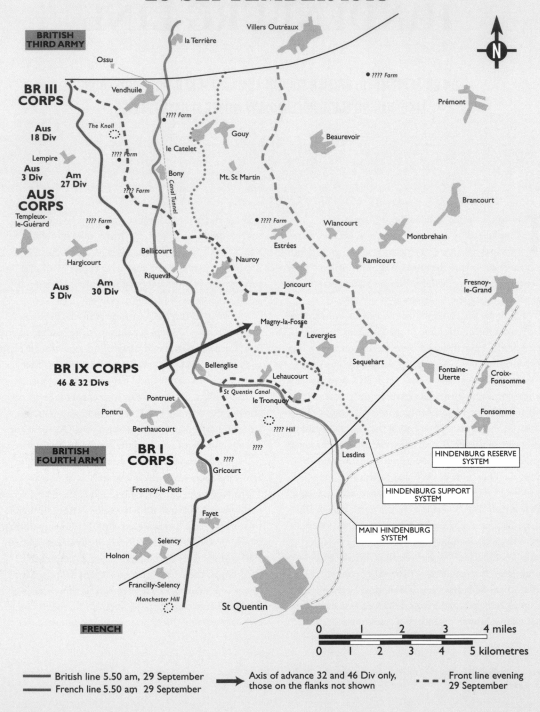

BRITISH
THIRD ARMY

Villers Outréaux

la Terrière

Ossu

BR III
CORPS

Vendhuile

???? Farm

Prémont

Aus
18 Div

The Knoll

???? Farm

Gouy

Beaurevoir

Lempire

le Catelet

Aus
3 Div

Am
27 Div

Bony

Mt. St Martin

AUS
CORPS

???? Farm

Brancourt

Templeux-
le-Guérard

???? Farm

Wiancourt

Montbrehain

Hargicourt

Bellicourt

???? Farm

Estrées

Ramicourt

Nauroy

Riqueval

Aus
5 Div

Am
30 Div

Joncourt

Fresnoy-
le-Grand

Magny-la-Fosse

BR IX CORPS
46 & 32 Divs

Bellenglise

Levergies

Sequehart

Fontaine-
Uterte

Croix-
Fonsomme

Lehaucourt

Pontruet

St Quentin Canal
le Tronquoy

Fonsomme

Pontru

Berthaucourt

???? Hill

????

HINDENBURG RESERVE
SYSTEM

BRITISH
FOURTH ARMY

BR I
CORPS

Lesdins

Gricourt

????

HINDENBURG SUPPORT
SYSTEM

Fresnoy-le-Petit

Fayet

MAIN HINDENBURG
SYSTEM

Selency

Holnon

Francilly-Selency

Manchester Hill

St Quentin

FRENCH

| 0 | 1 | 2 | 3 | 4 miles |
| 0 | 1 | 2 | 3 | 4 | 5 kilometres |

———— British line 5.50 am, 29 September

———— French line 5.50 am 29 September

⟶ Axis of advance 32 and 46 Div only,
those on the flanks not shown

- - - - Front line evening
29 September

Above: *Mark V tanks of 8th Battalion Tank Corps with infantry of the 5th Australian Division for its breaching the Hindenburg Line at Bellicourt. The "cribs" on top of some of the tanks are to drop into deep ditches to allow tanks to drive over them.*

1,000 yards without a creeping barrage. Unfortunately, the German machine-gunners and riflemen, not being neutralized by artillery, were able to lash the Americans with fire. In addition every one of the tanks in support of the Americans was knocked out by anti-tank artillery or ran onto mines in an old British minefield, which the tank crews were unaware of.

On the right the US 30th Division was far more successful, capturing the first two of the tunnel's defensive lines. The division eventually took the southern entrance to the tunnel, Bellicourt village, and part of the Hindenburg Line and Canal, but was then stopped. The Australian 4th Division passed through and, with tank support, advanced for several kilometres to the south-east. Eventually it made contact with the British 32nd Division, which had passed through the British 46th Division after

their brilliant attack on the Canal (see next chapter).

On the left – not even aerial reconnaissance could fix the position of the US 27th Division – the Australian 3rd Division was forced to pass through prematurely and fight its way forward with bombs and Lewis guns. The Australians were joined by groups of Americans (until the US 27th Division was withdrawn on 1 October). By then the Australians, with the British IX Corps, had captured the main Hindenburg Line. The final act was the Australian 2nd Division passing through the 3rd to take Montbrehain on 5 October. This was the final Australian ground action of the First World War. That evening, having handed over to the US II Corps, the Australians were withdrawn for a well-deserved rest; the war ended before they were needed again.

Left: *German troops surrendering to Australians.*

27

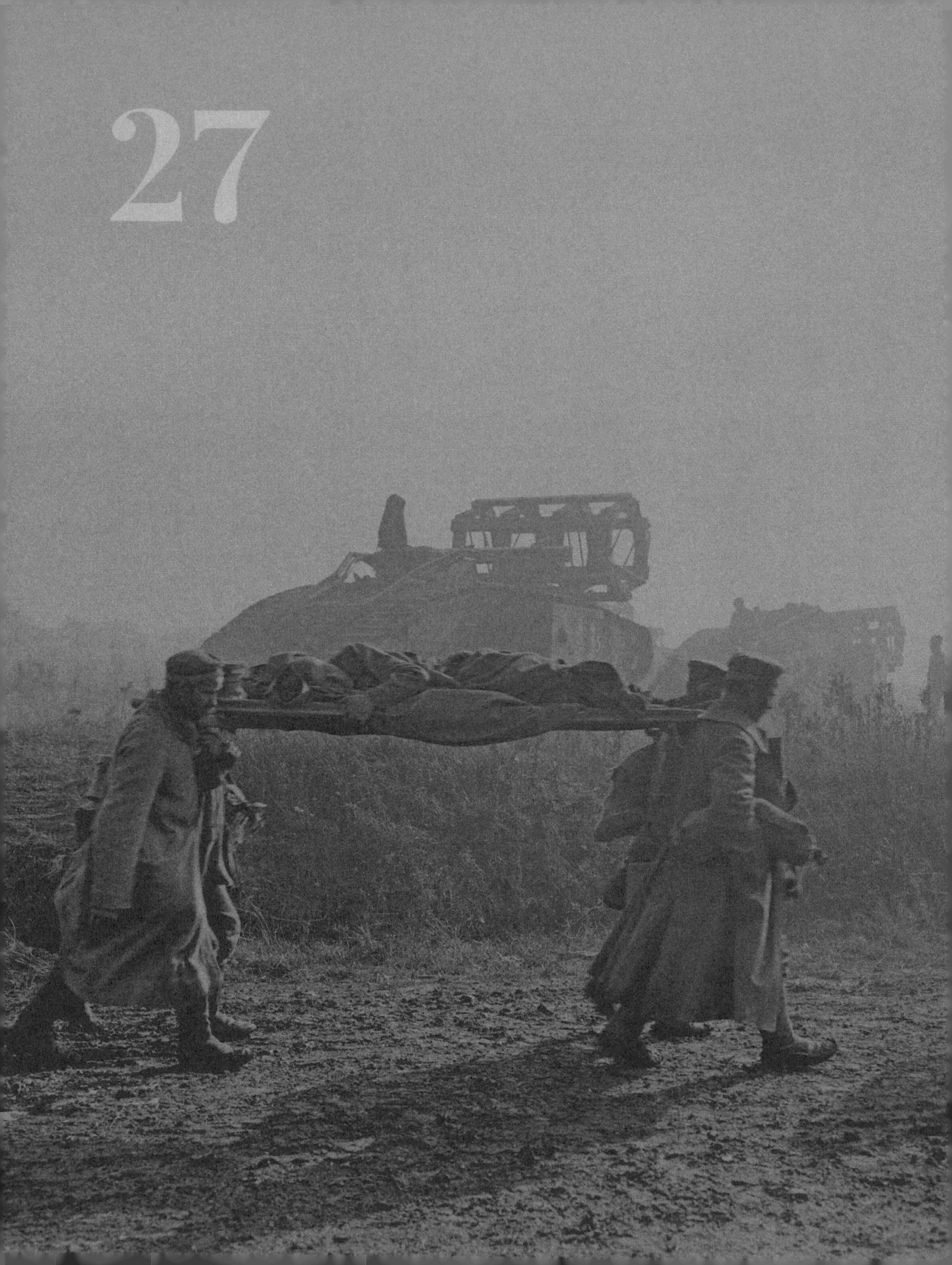

CROSSING THE ST QUENTIN CANAL

PART OF THE HINDENBURG LINE INCLUDED THE ADDITIONAL PROTECTION OF THE ST QUENTIN CANAL. THIS WAS THE OBSTACLE FACED BY THE BRITISH IX CORPS. "THE MERE SIGHT OF IT FROM OUR FRONT LINE TRENCHES INSPIRED RESPECT, AND MIGHT WELL HAVE CAUSED FEAR OF THE OUTCOME IN THE HEARTS OF ANY BUT THE STOUTEST SOLDIERS," RECORDED THE 46TH DIVISION HISTORIAN.

The canal at this point ran through a cutting with almost perpendicular sides, 30 to 50 feet high; in the northern part of the IX Corps sector, in front of Bellenglise, the water was six to eight feet deep; to the south it contained eight feet of mud. It was 35 feet wide, with barbed wire on the banks and along the bottom. Lieutenant General Sir John Monash had not included crossing the canal in his plan for breaching the Hindenburg Line. However, Lieutenant General Sir Walter Braithwaite, commanding IX Corps, produced a bold scheme to pass the 46th Division over the canal in front of Bellenglise, on the right of Monash's attack, subsequently passing the 32nd Division through the 46th to capture the main objective.

The preparations for the 46th Division attack were meticulous. The Germans must have been aware that an attack on the Hindenburg Line was in the offing, but it was possible to conceal the timing and the fact that the Bellenglise sector of the canal was to be included in the assault. Activity in the 46th Division sector had to be carefully concealed from the German air force, which was especially active over the British lines. The steep-sided canal was a formidable tank obstacle, so only 24 tanks were allocated to IX Corps

to be used in the second phase. The main fire support would be provided by artillery.

Some ingenious equipment was provided by the Royal Engineers: they constructed wooden piers for use as footbridges or rafts supported by empty petrol cans along with mud mats of canvas, lifelines, collapsible boats and scaling ladders. Some 3,000 lifebelts were requisitioned from cross-channel ferries. The Staffordshire Brigade tested all this equipment in a rehearsal on a château moat. They found that collapsible boats could be opened and launched in 20 seconds; fully loaded soldiers could swim across 40 yards of deep water in lifebelts; a man who could not swim could be pulled across on a line: all very encouraging.

On the day of the assault, 29 September 1918, fog descended over the battlefield. This suited the 46th Division perfectly, although it considerably hampered the Australian Corps on their northern flank. At 5.50 am, the 137th (Staffordshire) Infantry Brigade (Brigadier J.V. Campbell VC; 1st/5th South Staffordshires, 1st/6th South Staffordshires, 1st/6th North Staffordshires) led the 46th Division attack on the St Quentin Canal. The brigade, in small parties, keeping close to their artillery barrage and under the cover of the

---

Left: *Prisoners carry the wounded. Tanks with cribs in the background, 29 September 1918.*

fog, worked their way up to within a short distance of the enemy trenches and dashed in with the bayonet. The Germans fled in all directions.

Having reached the canal, the most testing time had arrived. The fog was still thick and provided welcome cover for the Staffordshires as they crossed the canal using the equipment provided by the Royal Engineers, suffering very few casualties in the process. They took 2,000 prisoners, more than their own numbers. They had every right to be pleased with themselves as, a few hours later, they lined the canal bank, some still wearing their lifejackets, to be congratulated by their brigade commander.

Meanwhile on cue, the other two brigades in the 46th Division passed through the Staffordshires and seized the next objectives. By 1.00 pm the mist had cleared, and the history of the 46th Division recorded:

> The sight was one for which every commander had lived during the long years of the war. As far as the eye could see, our troops were pushing forward; batteries were crossing the Canal and coming into action; engineers were everywhere at work; large bodies of prisoners were coming from all sides; and the men of the 32nd Division were advancing fast …" It was indeed a break-through. Thus the battle ended early in the afternoon with complete attainment of all objectives, and at 5.30 pm, the advanced troops of the 32nd Division passed through our lines in pursuit of the retreating enemy.

Right: The men of the 137th (Staffordshire) Infantry Brigade on the banks of the St Quentin Canal being addressed by their commander, Brigadier General J.C. Campbell VC on completion of the epic operation to cross the Canal.

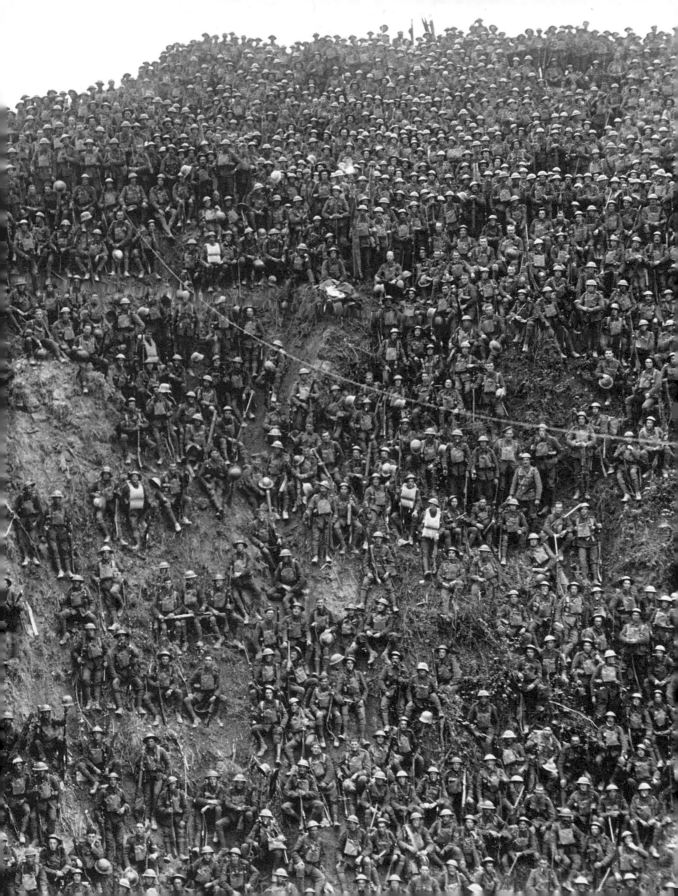

28

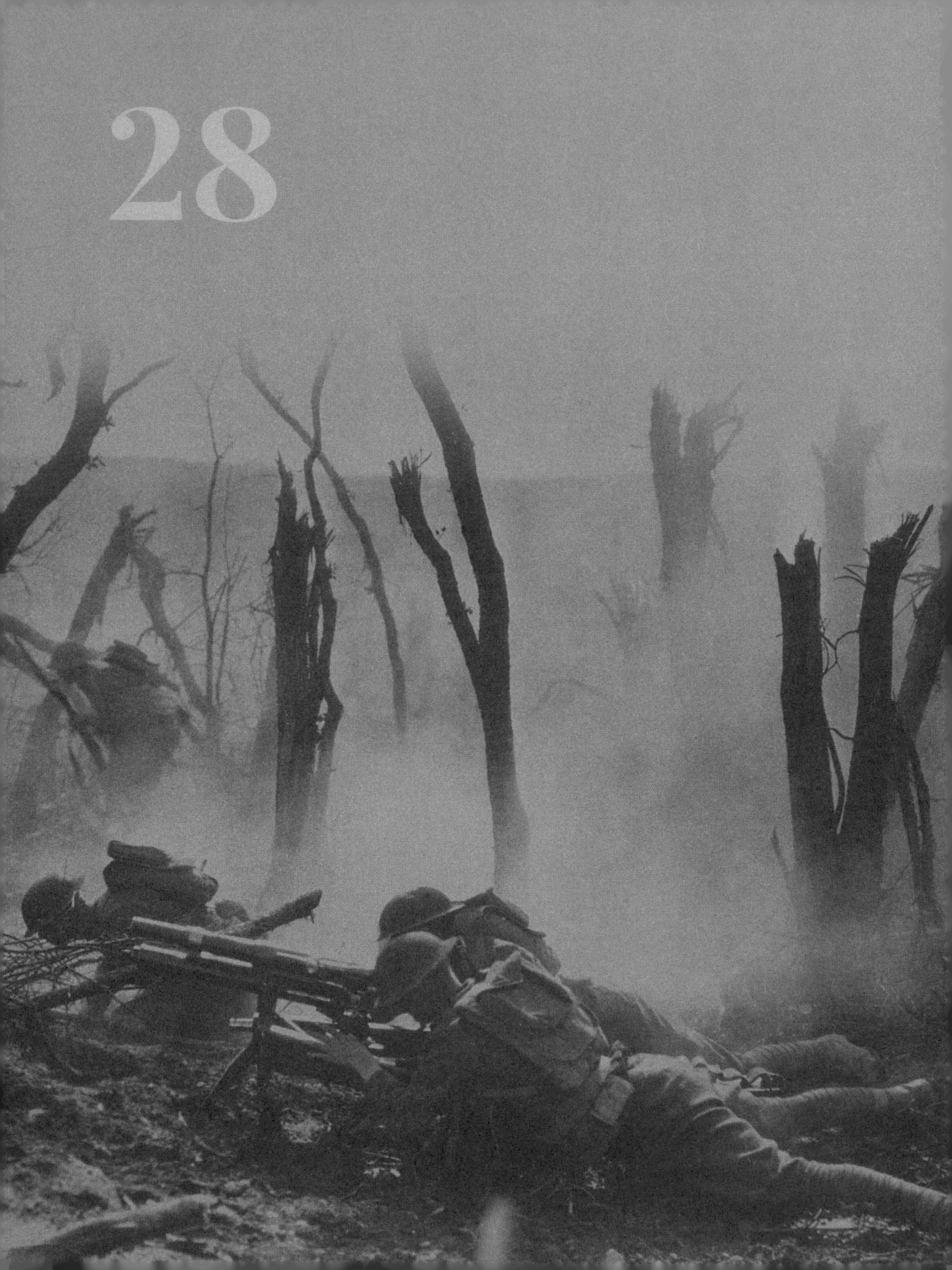

CHAMPAGNE AND BLANC MONT

GENERAL HENRI GOURAUD'S FRENCH FOURTH ARMY OFFENSIVE IN THE CHAMPAGNE GROUND TO A HALT IN LATE SEPTEMBER NEAR SOMME-PY.

At this stage the American 2nd Division found itself temporarily attached to French Fourth Army. Commanded by US Marine Major General John A. Lejeune, this elite division consisting of the US Marine 4th Brigade and the US Army's 3rd Infantry Brigade was now the most experienced American formation in France. The vital ground in the Fourth Army's sector was Blanc Mont Ridge, held by the Germans since 1914, which had resisted all attempts by the French to capture it. When the 2nd Division joined the Fourth Army, the French staff suggested that the big American brigades be broken up and distributed round the badly understrength French formations. With a strength of 3,600 of all ranks, a US Marine or US Army regiment was equivalent to a British brigade. Each regiment had three battalions each about 1,100 strong, plus a regimental machine-gun company, headquarters and supply companies. A US Marine or Infantry brigade was over twice the size of its British equivalent. Lejeune, horrified at the notion of splitting up his formation, appealed to Gouraud: keep the 2nd Division together and he would capture Blanc Mont. Gouraud agreed, and on 29 September Lejeune was ordered to launch his attack on 3 October.

The Marine Brigade was to attack on the left, with the Army 3rd Infantry Brigade angling in on the right. Meanwhile the French would attack Essen Hill. An intermediate objective for the Marines was the ominously named *Bois de la Vipère* (Viper Woods). In accordance with Lejeune's orders, with the aim of maintaining surprise, there was no lengthy preliminary artillery barrage, just five minutes of high intensity shelling by 200 guns, before the 6th Marine Regiment attacked. Attached to the 6th Marines, and also to 5th Marines who were following up the attack, were French tanks.

In under three hours the assaulting companies of 1st and 2nd Battalions 6th Marines (1st/6th and 2nd/6th) were firing Verey light signals to say that they had secured the objective. Meanwhile, Number 17 Company of 5th Marines found itself fighting a private war in what was actually French "real estate", dealing with German machine-gunners on the eastern end of Essen Hill, a French responsibility, which the French had failed to take. Having handed over the position after the French eventually arrived, the 5th Marines had to do the job all over again because the French lost the position to a German counter-attack.

The advance of the 6th Marines secured the top of Blanc Mont, except its western slope in the French sector, which the French had failed to take. The Marine Brigade was now around two miles into enemy territory, with an open flank all the way back to Essen Hill. To plug this dangerous gap, and to try to neutralize the German

---

Left: *American machine-gunner supporting infantry in wooded terrain somewhere in the Argonne.*

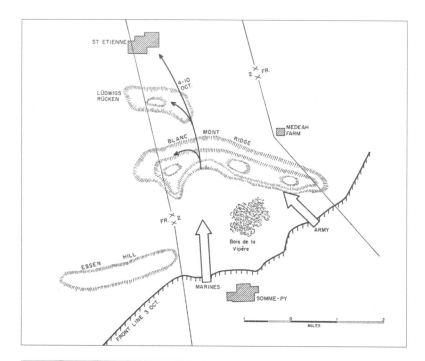

St. Etienne

4-10 OCT.

2 × FR.

LÜDWIGS RÜCKEN

MEDEAH FARM

BLANC MONT RIDGE

FR. × 2

Bois de la Vipère

ARMY

ESSEN HILL

MARINES

SOMME-PY

FRONT LINE 3 OCT.

MILES

Below: *One of the German positions on Blanc Mont. The wire netting over the trench is to impede attackers.*

Right: *American troops in trenches. They could either be standing-to for an attack or waiting to assault.*

MAJOR GENERAL JOHN A. LEJEUNE USMC

Major General John A. Lejeune photographed after the war, with the 2nd Division patch on his left arm. Lejeune was commissioned into the United States Marine Corps in 1890. He first saw action in the Spanish-American War of 1898, and subsequently took part in the Cuban, Puerto Rican and Philippine campaigns, as well as in Mexico and the Battle of Veracruz. In June 1918 he took command of the 32nd US Army Division, but soon took over the 4th Marine Brigade, part of the 2nd Division. On 28 July 1918 he assumed command of the 2nd Division, remaining in command until August 1919, when the division was demobilized. He was the second marine to hold an army divisional command. The only other marine to do so held the command for two weeks.

machine-gunners, the 5th Marines took up positions almost at right angles to the axis of advance – a military manoeuvre known as "refusing a flank", in this case the left flank.

At dawn on 4 October, the 5th Marines passed through the 6th Marines and headed for St Étienne. The 6th Marines redeployed to guard the left flank and engaged the 80 or so German machine-gunners that were holding up the French from positions on the western slopes of Blanc Mont. By midday, when 3rd/5th Marines were within 1,000 yards of St Étienne, a German counter-attack began to come in. The reserve battalion, the 1st/5th Marines swung half left and charged the Germans, with no artillery support. Despite being heavily shelled, the Marines pushed the Germans back to St Étienne. A little more than 100 men out of around 1000 1st/5th Marines were still fit to fight after this remarkable feat. For the next three days, the Marine Brigade slogged forward, finally entering St Étienne on 8 October. The French XI Corps at last came up on their left. The Germans mounted one more counter attack, held off by two companies of 6th Marines, one commanded by a sergeant, the senior survivor. The battle for Blanc Mont cost 2,538 Marines killed or wounded. In one company, 230 rations were sent forward based on the company's last reported ration strength. Twenty-two officers and enlisted men were alive to eat them.

Right: *American soldiers passing through the ruins of Varennes, during the Argonne offensive.*

29

ALLIED ADVANCE – CAMBRAI AND LE CATEAU

IN OCTOBER THE ALLIED ADVANCE BEGAN TO GAIN MOMENTUM – THOUGH NOT IN DRAMATIC LEAPS FORWARD, GAINING SCORES OF MILES EACH DAY, AS WAS COMMONPLACE IN THE NEXT BIG WAR AND IN SOME CAMPAIGNS THEREAFTER.

But in October and early November, gains were being made almost every day. Sometimes the fighting was hard, with German counter-attacks as dangerous as ever. On other occasions the Allies would encounter a scattered line of posts manned by rear guards that did not stay long to fight it out. In truth Germany was exhausted. Their casualties just in 1918 were enormous, including a quarter of a million men taken prisoner that year. The war had lasted for over four years; the Germans were losing, with little prospect of turning the situation around.

The Allied advance began again on 8 October on the fronts of the French First Army and British Fourth and Third Armies; the ensuing series of engagements is called the Second Battle of Cambrai because the town fell the next day. It was not a pushover: the Germans fought hard and counter-attacked frequently. The Germans managed to knock out several British tanks both with field artillery firing point blank, and with their own and captured tanks. Some of the toughest fighting was experienced in Third Army's XVII Corps, by the British 63rd (Royal Naval) Division, which included a Royal Marine Brigade, and was rated as one of the best formations in the BEF. On 8 October the 63rd (RN)

Division took 1,189 prisoners at a cost of 703 casualties. In Fourth Army the best effort was by the American 30th Division. The Americans took over 1,500 prisoners and 30 guns from a total of four German divisions they fought that day. The Fourth Army's "bag" that day was over 4,000 prisoners and 56 guns.

Above: *A Royal Field Artillery battery passing through Pronville during the attack on Cambrai, 27 September 1918.*

Left: *Battle of Cambrai. Men of the 20th Battalion, Manchester Regiment (25th Division) resting by a tank (serial number 9891), disabled by side-slipping down a railway embankment. Near Prémont, 8 October 1918.*

On 9 October, German resistance consisted mainly of rear guards, and by the end of that day the Third Army patrols linked up with the Canadians in Cambrai. The town was deserted and on fire. Haig noted in his diary:

It was only yesterday that the Enemy was driven from this great fortress, and yet I was able to walk about today, 24 hours later, almost out of hearing of the guns. The dead were still lying about and one was able to see where the struggle had been fiercest … how our gallant fellows had pushed through …

The Germans were retreating on the whole front of the Fourth, Third and First Armies, and also that of the French First Army on their right. Ahead of these formations lay open fields and undamaged villages, large farms and woods thick with trees, very different from the Western Front vista that endures in public perception to this day: a sea of mud and shell craters with the occasional sparse bristle of shattered tree stumps among coils of rusting barbed wire. Now was the time for pursuit. But the traditional pursuit arm, the cavalry, could not cope on this front by itself, and the tanks available

Below: *Capture of Cambrai by the British 57th Division. Soldiers of the Loyal North Lancashire Regiment on return from a patrol in Cambrai, 9 October 1918.*

Above: *Capture of Cambrai by the British 57th Division. Soldiers of the Loyal North Lancashire Regiment wearing* Pickelhaubes *which they found whilst on patrol in Cambrai, 9 October 1918.*

were not weapons of pursuit. The day of a truly mobile arm had yet to arrive. Horsed cavalry was almost obsolete and "blitzkrieg" armoured formations would only emerge 20 years later. The generals were in the unenviable position of having to fight a war in an era of a technology gap. An advance of five miles a day was good, eight or ten very good. But even this, after four years in which advances of a few hundred yards were hailed as major victories, was progress indeed. Although the Cavalry Corps made several attempts to cut through to the enemy rear and cause havoc, only infantry and artillery could overcome the German rear guards, or occasionally, Whippet tanks would be enough to persuade them to scuttle back.

There was one exception to this: when the Canadian Cavalry Brigade assisted the 66th Division in Fourth

Army at Clary and the Bois de Gattigny. Lord Strathcona's Horse and the Fort Garry Horse carried out a series of successful charges supported by the Royal Canadian Horse Artillery. The remaining enemy were mopped up by the South African Brigade of the 66th Division. The Canadians, exploiting success, pushed on until they reached the outskirts of Le Cateau. The last time the BEF had been in this vicinity was during the retreat from Mons in 1914.

At this stage the British Fifth and Second Armies, and the Belgian/French forces at the northern end of the line, had made no progress, and were preparing for a new offensive. In the Argonne, the American First Army and French Fourth Army were still hammering the enemy, but had made little progress since 4 October.

Left: *Battle of Cambrai. Troops of the 10th Battalion, Duke of Cornwall's Light Infantry, the Pioneers of the British 2nd Division, building a pontoon across the canalized Scheldt river, 8 October 1918. There are German prisoners with them.*

PART 9
AN END TO WAR

ALLIED ADVANCE – LILLE, SELLE AND SAMBRE

THE LAST WEEKS OF THE WAR IN THE BRITISH AND AMERICAN SECTORS SAW ALMOST CONTINUOUS ACTION. THE AMERICANS BATTLED THROUGH THE THICK COUNTRY OF THE ARGONNE WITH INTERMITTENT HELP FROM THE FRENCH FOURTH ARMY.

Meanwhile the British followed up a retreating enemy, fighting him when he stood at bay. The French First Army on the British right was not in a state to provide much assistance. Not surprisingly the French were worn out. Between 1 July and 15 September they had suffered 279,000 casualties. Add these to around 245,000 lost in the battles to stem the German offensive in the spring, and the "butcher's bill" was a horrific 524,000.

The BEF, along with its allies, was now fighting a new style of war. Paradoxically, much would not have been "new" to the old professional soldiers of the 1914 BEF. Their training had reflected hard-won British experience in South Africa – how to move over open ground, how best to use cover, the best methods of firing, moving and marksmanship. This was utterly alien to officers and soldiers who had become accustomed to three and a half years of tightly controlled, minutely rehearsed, limited advances some measured in yards and over familiar ground, which on the whole required little tactical sense.

Now tactical awareness was hugely important. This loaded much responsibility on commanders from young battalion COs, company and platoon commanders, right down to corporals commanding sections. An engagement could be won or lost by the actions of these men. It was a situation familiar to anyone who has fought in a modern battle, articulated by the general who said: "many a battle has been won by a junior commander, all the general has to do is put him where he can win it for him."

On the left of the BEF, General Sir Herbert Plumer's Second Army and General Sir William Birdwood's Fifth Army made good progress. On 14 October Plumer advanced well beyond Lille, which forced Crown Prince Rupprecht to abandon the city. On 17 October, the Fifth Army patrols walked into Lille, finding it almost undamaged. The citizens of Lille greeted the British ecstatically. Further south, the Fourth, Third and First Armies were also gaining ground. On 17 October, the Fourth Army attacked along the line of the River

Previous page: *British official entry into Lille. Infantry Regiment of the 47th Division in the procession, 28 October 1918. Note the extemporized Allied flags attached to the bayonets provided in large numbers by the inhabitants.*

Left: *Official entry into Lille. The Mayor, the Bishop, prominent citizens of the city; Fifth Army, XI Corps, and 47th Divisional commanders; and a large gathering of officers and civilians, (including the British Secretary of State for War, Winston Churchill) on the grandstand at the march past of the 47th Division, 28 October 1918.*

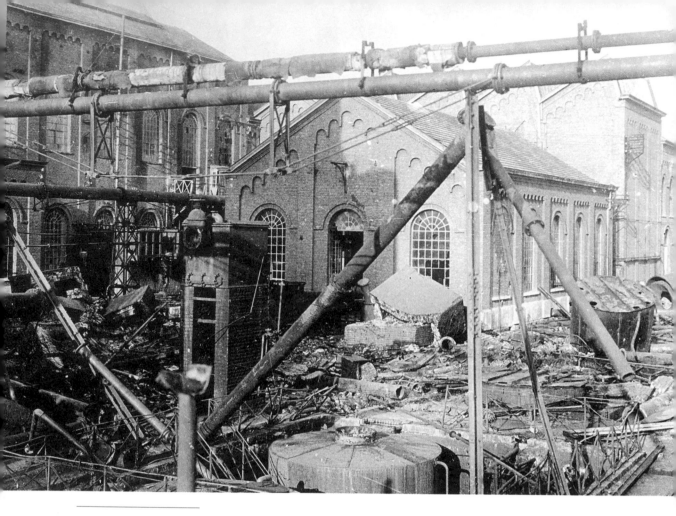

Above:: *The Cockerill-Sambre steelworks at Seraing, destroyed by the German Army.*

Selle, while the Third Army extended the battle to the north and the First Army advanced six miles. Despite the weather, the RAF continued to support ground troops. The official history comments: "… the targets which streamed towards the bottleneck into Germany were innumerable … the setting was such as to ensure the most awesome effects for the employment of air power …"

The Fourth Army's Battle of the Selle reached its crescendo on 23 October in some very tough fighting. British tank losses were heavy, and the burden of the battle devolved on the infantry, and of course on the junior commanders, as shown by the last sentence of the Victoria Cross citation for Lieutenant Frederick Hedges attached to the 6th Battalion the Northamptonshire Regiment: "The direct result of this officer's action was

that the whole front line which had been held up since the morning was enabled to advance, thus having a great effect on subsequent operations."

The Battle of the Selle ended on 24 October. It had involved three British armies: 24 British and two American divisions had overcome 31 German divisions, netting 20,000 prisoners and 475 guns. But the Germans were still fighting, and delaying the Allied advance with their customary skill, led by resolute commanders. On 31 October, Haig recorded in his diary: "The Enemy is fighting a very good rear guard action and all are agreed that from a military standpoint, the Enemy has not yet been sufficiently beaten as to cause him to accept an ignominious peace. Neither on our right or on our left are the French Armies really fighting …"

On 4 November, what turned out to be the last great offensive began with the British Fourth, Third and First Armies attacking on a front of 40 miles. Ahead of them lay the Sambre–Oise Canal and the Sambre River, as well as the thick woodland of the Forest of Mormal. The Fourth Army crossed the Sambre–Oise Canal and carved out a bridgehead 15 miles long and around three deep. The Third Army advanced five miles, while the First Army kept pressing on. The German retreat gathered momentum. Nonetheless there was little sign that they were cracking. But Ludendorff had cracked.

On 25 October, he recorded: "On the evening of the 25th [of October] the Western Front was enduring the greatest strain. There was fighting from the Dutch frontier to Verdun. No more help was coming from home. Not a word of encouragement was given. It was miraculous that the troops fought so heroically."

On 27 October at an audience with the Kaiser, Ludendorff resigned, saying that he no longer enjoyed the Kaiser's confidence, and begged most humbly to be relieved of his office. He added, "His Majesty accepted my resignation."

Below: *Troops of the 8th Battalion, Liverpool Regiment (57th British Division, XI Corps), accompanied by local children, entering Lille, 18 October 1918. The soldier carrying a Lewis machine gun is Private Arthur John O'Hare 307465.*

Below: *The Aulnoye–Le Quesnoy railway line bridge over the River Sambre at Aulnoye, demolished by the Germans.*

ARMISTICE

ON 10 NOVEMBER 1918, TROOPS OF THE 4TH AND 7TH CANADIAN BRIGADES WERE ENGAGED WITH REAR GUARDS OF THE GERMAN SEVENTEENTH ARMY ON THE OUTSKIRTS OF MONS.

At about 5.00 pm, the Germans pulled out, and early next morning the Canadians entered the town. Here the BEF had first fought the Germans in 1914 at the beginning of the war. This was the day it would end: 11 November 1918.

To get a sense of the events leading up to this point, we must rewind to 28 September 1918, the day Ludendorff and Hindenburg agreed that Germany should request an armistice. The German government agreed and asked President Wilson to start negotiations. In approaching Wilson, the Germans hoped to obtain easier terms than from the French and British, who they calculated were more likely to be in a more vengeful mood and demand stiffer terms in payment for the blood and treasure they had expended in over four years. On 8 October the Americans replied asking for clarification on certain aspects of the German proposals for peace. The exchanges of notes continued for nearly three weeks. General Pershing, along with some senior British commanders, was wary of concluding peace terms while German armies were everywhere occupying foreign soil. He felt that doing so would open the way for the Germans to claim that their armies had not been beaten. This is, of course, exactly what happened. Many Germans, including Adolf Hitler, propagated the myth of the "the stab in the army's back" by socialists and Jews that had brought about the defeat of Germany. Hitler was not the creator of this nonsense. German generals fomented it before the war

Above: *Foch, second from right, outside his railway carriage after signing the Armistice. On his right, Admiral Sir Rosslyn Wemyss, British First Sea Lord (head of the British Delegation). To his right, Foch's chief of staff, General Weygand, who as Commander-in-Chief of the French Army, in 1940 signed the Armistice with the victorious Germans in exactly the same place.*

Left: *A mutinous sailor (foreground, right) joins the crowd in Germany.*

ended to shift the blame for defeat away from the army and cover up their strategic incompetence.

Meanwhile in Germany, there were daily strikes and food riots. Admiral Franz von Hipper, commanding the German High Seas Fleet, planned to sortie into the North Sea on 29 October in a desperate attempt to engage the combined British and American Grand Fleet. Most of his ship's companies viewed this as a "death ride" and refused to sail. This was soon followed by a mutiny by the crews of most of the capital ships in the High Seas Fleet. By 9 November the navy could no longer be relied on. The next day, the Kaiser abdicated. The creation of a German fleet by this deeply flawed man had not caused the First World War, but when it broke out, the fleet's existence ensured that Great Britain would be on the side of Germany's enemies. Now his beloved fleet had deserted him.

Meanwhile a German delegation was meeting with an Allied delegation led by Marshal Foch in his headquarters railway carriage at Compiègne to discuss armistice terms.

Below left:: *Ex-Kaiser Wilhelm II crosses the border into Holland after abdicating and fleeing from Germany.*

Below right: *"aaa" in the "signalese" of the time stood for "full stop".*

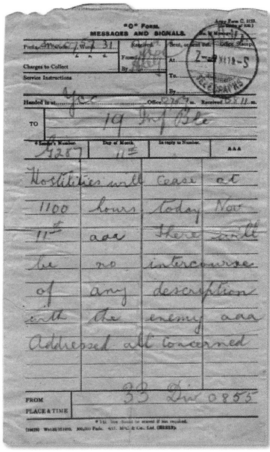

Above: *Captain A.W.L. Paget MC and Second Lieutenant P.R.J. Barry MC of the 1st Battalion Irish Guards reading news of the Armistice to their men at Maubeuge.*

The terms demanded that:

1. The Germans evacuate all occupied territory
2. Huge quantities of military equipment be handed over to the Allies
3. All German land west of the Rhine be de-militarized
4. The Allies establish three bridgeheads over the Rhine
5. All U-boats be surrendered
6. The most modern ships in the German navy be interned
7. The Treaty of Brest-Litovsk be annulled
8. All German troops in Eastern Europe be withdrawn behind the German frontier of 1914

At the Armistice Conference, the German delegates quibbled over some of the points. At which point Foch replied: "I would remind you that this is a military armistice, that the war is not ended thereby, and that it is directed at preventing your nation from continuing the war. You must recollect the reply given by Bismarck in 1871 … Bismarck then said '*Krieg ist Krieg*', and I say to you '*la guerre est la guerre*'." At 10.30 pm on 10 November, the German delegates received a telegram from the Reich Chancellor authorizing them to sign the terms of the Armistice as submitted. The news was passed in a variety of ways to the troops.

One officer, Lieutenant Harold Horne of First Battalion Royal Marine Light Infantry, recalled:

During the night of 10/11 [November] the front line was NE of the village of Bougnies. About 6.0 am we got orders that an armistice would take effect from 11.0 am when hostilities would cease and all units would remain stationary on the line then reached.

Above: *Crowds outside Buckingham Palace on 11 November 1918.*

The advance started at 7.00 am in a NE direction … to Villers St Ghislain (four miles SE of Mons) …

At 11 o'clock when we halted, an enemy rearguard who had been firing from a wood a few hundred yards in front sent up some coloured flares – a *feu de joie* at the ending of the war.

Another officer, Captain Arnold Thompson, the Brigade Major (chief of staff) of the 19th Infantry Brigade, was handed a pink form containing a message from 33rd Division, reproduced on the previous page. The 33rd Division, part of V Corps, Third Army, had been in reserve near Maubeuge since 8 November following the Battle of the Sambre. On 9 November there had been rumours of an Armistice, and the Division ran a one-franc sweepstake on the result. At 12 noon on 11 November, the Divisional Band paraded in the streets of Aulnoye and played the Marseillaise and 'God Save the King'. The 33rd Division (which included the 19th Infantry Brigade), had been advancing since 18 September 1918, and between that date and 11 November 1918 had suffered 931 killed in action, 6,005 wounded, and 640 missing (the majority would subsequently be found to have been killed).

Above: *Crowds in Paris on Armistice Day 1918.*

32

VERSAILLES

MARSHAL FOCH MEANT EXACTLY WHAT HE SAID WHEN HE TOLD THE GERMAN DELEGATION IN HIS RAILWAY CARRIAGE HEADQUARTERS THAT "THIS IS A MILITARY ARMISTICE, THAT THE WAR IS NOT ENDED THEREBY, AND THAT IT IS DIRECTED AT PREVENTING YOUR NATION FROM CONTINUING THE WAR."

Part of that prevention included the demand that 10 German battleships, all six battle cruisers, eight light cruisers, and 50 of the most modern destroyers would be interned at a designated Allied port. It was agreed that this would be at Scapa Flow in the Orkneys – the base for the British Grand Fleet through most of the war. Admiral Sir David Beatty, Commander-in-Chief Grand Fleet, was determined that the internment should carry all the features of a surrender, which it was not. For the internment of the High Seas Fleet was the direct result of the great victory won in France by the French, American and above all the five British Armies. The German High Seas Fleet had not been beaten in battle, but cowed into a state of sullen dejection following its encounter with the Grand Fleet at Jutland in 1916. Sea power exerted by the Royal Navy enabled Britain and her allies to win the war. Without the Royal Navy the five Armies of the BEF, and later the American Army, would not have been transported to France, reinforced, built up and kept supplied. France's armies alone were incapable of defeating the Germans. Britain was the linchpin of the Entente Alliance, a pin that could only be kept in place by sea power. The Royal Navy was the sure shield that enabled the Allies to win the war. The U-boats nearly overcame the shield, but convoys were introduced in the nick of time. Without the Royal Navy, the Allies would have lost the war.

On 21 November 1918, Beatty took his entire fleet to sea: 33 battleships (including the 6th American Battle Squadron), nine battle cruisers, 27 cruisers, and all the Grand Fleet destroyer flotillas, together with ships from Dover, Harwich and the Channel ports, a total of 370 ships and 90,000 men. Led by the cruiser *Cardiff*, they steamed out of the Firth of Forth, the mass of ships at 18 knots taking nearly four hours to pass May Island at the mouth of the Forth. As they met the German ships, the Grand Fleet turned, formed into a double line each side of the German ships, and escorted the High Seas Fleet into captivity.

The treaty signed in the Hall of Mirrors in the Palace of Versailles on 28 June 1919 officially ended the First World War. The venue itself was especially symbolic for France. Here, on 18 January 1871, following the humiliating defeat of France in the Franco-Prussian war, the German Empire had been proclaimed, consisting of Prussia and all other German states. King Wilhelm of Prussia assumed the German imperial crown. This manifestation of what Sir Edward Grey once called "Germany's itch to dominate", staged in a palace built by one of France's greatest kings, Louis XIV, rubbed salt into France's wounds. The French had never forgotten, and there were still many men in influential positions who had witnessed and participated in the Franco-Prussian war. Now, 47 years later, it was payback time.

Left: *German troops being welcomed home by a large crowd. Scenes like this helped foster the myth that the German Army was not defeated in the field but stabbed in the back by dissident elements in Germany.*

The Treaty deprived Germany of 13.5 per cent of its 1914 territory, about 13 per cent of its economic resources, about seven million people and all its overseas possessions. Alsace and Lorraine, wrenched away by the Germans in 1871, were restored to France. The Rhineland and mining district of the Saarland were placed under Allied occupation for 15 years. Parts of East Prussia were handed to Lithuania and a reconstituted Poland. The latter had not existed since the Seven Years' War in the mid eighteenth century. A corridor carved through East Prussia to the former German port of Danzig gave Poland access to the Baltic, but cut East Prussia off from the rest of Germany. Military clauses included restricting the German Army to 100,000 men, and prohibiting conscription, heavy artillery, tanks, gas, aircraft or airships. The German navy was restricted to vessels under 10,000 tons, and forbidden to possess submarines or aircraft. The treaty also assigned war guilt to Germany and used this as a basis for imposing payment of reparations.

Liberal Allied opinion deemed the treaty to be too harsh, while others considered it too lenient. The treaty was rejected by Congress in the USA – demonstrating lack of support for President Wilson – and thus began a period of isolationism on the part of America. The USA withdrew from involvement in European affairs, with dire consequences for peace in Europe. The most virulent

ADMIRAL DAVID BEATTY

Beatty, an officer for whom the term "laid back" might have been invented, did not initially shine (except as a polo player in Malta in the late 1880s). He first achieved fame aged 25 commanding a gunboat on the Nile in the 1896 Sudan Campaign where he won a DSO, and was marked out for promotion. Subsequently, Beatty was wounded while fighting ashore during the Boxer Rebellion in China in 1900. He was promoted to Captain aged 29 (the average was 42). In 1901, he hazarded his career by the then socially damaging step of marrying a divorcee. When he damaged his first command, HMS *Juno*, his American millionaire wife telegraphed the Admiralty offering to buy a replacement. He was, however, a highly successful captain of four warships in succession. He was promoted to Rear Admiral in 1910 – at 38 years old, the youngest since Nelson. In 1912 Churchill, then First Lord of the Admiralty, selected him as his Private Naval Secretary. In 1913 he was appointed to the plum job of commanding the First Battle Cruiser Squadron (BCS). In 1914, with the addition of the Second and Third BCS to his existing command, Beatty became Vice-Admiral Battle Cruiser Fleet and a Knight Commander of the Bath. He commanded the Battle Cruiser Fleet at the Battles of Helgoland, Dogger Bank and Jutland. He took over command of the Grand Fleet from Admiral Sir John Jellicoe in November 1916.

Above: *L-R: Italian Prime Minister Vittorio Orlando, British Prime Minister David Lloyd George, French Prime Minister Georges Clemenceau and President of the United States Woodrow Wilson in Paris for the peace treaty signed at Versailles.*

critics of the treaty were right-wing elements in Germany, of whom the National Socialists, or Nazis, under Adolf Hitler would become the most outspoken and malevolent. Led by Hitler, who as a corporal had been awarded the Iron Cross for his bravery in the First World War, Germany instigated the Second a mere 21 years after the end of the First.

Debate about the flaws in the treaty, and about the outcome of the various settlements of territory and peoples in the ensuing years, continue to this day. Whole books have been written on the subject. Space does not allow further discussion here. Our purpose is to show how the Entente Allies won the First World War.

Above: *The German battleships* Seydlitz, Moltke, Hindenburg, Derfflinger *and* Von Der Tann, *leading the German High Seas Fleet ships into the Firth of Forth to be interned. British Airship NS8 flies overhead.*

GLOSSARY

Battalion – see **Regiment**. An infantry battalion in the British and Dominion Armies was supposed to consist of 30 officers and 977 other ranks, a total of 1,007. By 1918 it was very rare to find a battalion at this strength. Commanded by a lieutenant colonel, an infantry battalion consisted of a headquarters and four rifle companies. Each company was supposed to consist of 227, all ranks commanded by a captain or major, and divided into four platoons. A platoon at full strength, commanded by a lieutenant or second lieutenant, consisted of two sergeants, three corporals, and 48 soldiers in four sections, each commanded by a non-commissioned officer (NCO).

BEF – British Expeditionary Force, the collective title for the British armies on the Western Front under the command of Field Marshal Sir Douglas Haig. The BEF included large contingents from the Dominion of Canada, the Commonwealth of Australia, the Dominion of New Zealand, the Union of South Africa, Newfoundland, and the Colonies. In 1914 an Indian corps of two infantry divisions and a cavalry brigade served on the Western Front, but by 1918, most Indian troops were serving in the Middle East. By 1918, the BEF consisted of five armies. Each army, commanded by a full general, consisted of two or more corps. A corps, commanded by a lieutenant general, comprised two or more divisions. Corps and divisions were not permanently assigned to a particular army, but moved to where they were needed. The extract below from the Order of Battle of the BEF in France on 27 September 1918 is a "snapshot" of the organization of just the First Army on that day, and how divisions came and went. "Snapshots" of the other four armies give a similar picture of their orders of battle.

> First Army (General Sir Henry Horne)
> > VII Corps (Lieutenant General Sir Aylmer Hunter-Weston)
> > > 8th Division
> > > 20th Division
> > > 20th Division
> > > 24th Division (to Third Army 30 September)
> > > 49th Division (to XXII Corps 10 October)
> > > > 12th Division (from Fourth Army 4 October)
> > > > 52nd Division (from Third Army 10 October)
> > > > 58th Division (from Fourth Army 30 September; to Fifth Army 14 October)

> XXII Corps (Lieutenant General Sir Alexander Godley)
> > 4th Division (with Canadian Corps from 27 September to 7 October)
> > 51st Division
> > 56th Division (to Canadian Corps 11 October)
> > > 11th Division (from Canadian Corps 13 October)
> > > 49th Division (from VIII Corps 10 October)

> Canadian Corps (Lieutenant General Sir Arthur Currie)
> > 1st Canadian Division (reserve to XXII Corps from 7 October)
> > 2nd Canadian Division
> > 3rd Canadian Division
> > 11th Division (to XXII Corps 13 October)
> > > 56th Division (from XXII Corps 11 October)

Brigade – commanded by a brigadier general, an infantry brigade consisted of a headquarters and three infantry battalions (cut from four battalions – except in Australian, Canadian and New Zealand brigades which maintained four battalions per brigade – see Introduction, page 10). The rank of brigadier general was replaced after the First World War by brigadier, who is not a general officer.

Corps – although divisions might come and go from one corps to another according to circumstance, a corps was a permanently constituted formation consisting of:
> Headquarters
> Corps Cavalry
> Headquarters Corps Heavy Artillery
> Heavy Trench Mortar Battery
> Cyclist Battalion
> Sharpshooters Group
> Corps Signal Troops
> Corps Motor Transport Column
> Heavy Artillery Army Service Corps Company
> Medium Ordnance Mobile Workshop
> Light Ordnance Mobile Workshop

Division – the order of battle of a division was:

Headquarters

Three Infantry Brigades each of three battalions
(Australians, Canadians and New Zealanders had
four battalions in a brigade)

One Heavy Trench Mortar Battery (Canadian divisions had
two)

Two Artillery Brigades each of three 18-pdr, and one 4.5-in
howitzer batteries

Three Trench Mortar Batteries

Ammunition Column

Three Field Companies Royal Engineers

Signal Company

Pioneer Battalion

Machine Gun Battalion

Divisional Train (four companies Army Service Corps –
this was not a railway train but lorry companies for
moving supplies by road)

Three Field Ambulances (these were medical units of
doctors, nurses and orderlies, not just ambulance
vehicles, although these were included)

Mobile Veterinary Section

GAC – *Groupe d'armées du Centre* (French Army Group Centre).

GAE – *Groupe d' armées de L'Est* (French Army Group East).

GAR – *Groupe d' armées de Réserve* (French Army Group Reserve).

GHQ – British General Headquarters.

GQG – *Grand Quarter Général* (French General Headquarters).

Hindenburg Line – the British name for the series of
fortifications along the line Lens–Noyon–Reims started by the
Germans in winter 1916 and known to them as the Siegfried
line. The Hindenburg Line was designed to provide defence in
depth consisting of: an initial large anti-tank ditch behind which
there were at least five barriers of barbed wire; next a line of forts
and blockhouses containing machine guns, and finally a series
of trenches dug in zigzags to provide enfilading fire. Two lines
of artillery were sited in rear, usually in reverse slope positions
wherever possible, and sometimes in trenches and tunnels.
Eventually the "line" was 300 miles long, consisting of five
major defensive positions (Flanders, Wotan, Siegfried, Hunding,
Kriemhild and Michel).

Regiment – originally a regiment in the British army was of
horse or foot, raised by command of the King or Queen, and
later Parliament, and named after its colonel, usually a royal
appointee. By the First World War the regiment had become
the basic organization in the British and Dominion Armies
for cavalry units. In the case of the infantry, the British Army
battalion belongs to a regiment, of which in this war there
could be several battalions. An infantry regiment in the British,
and Dominion service, did not fight as a unit. The various
battalions of a particular regiment could be found in different
divisions or even in different theatres of war. When war broke
out, each infantry regiment (except the Foot Guards), consisted
of two regular battalions, and a number of Territorial Army
and militia battalions (we would now call them 'reservists'). On
the outbreak of war more battalions were raised. For example
the Durham Light Infantry raised 42 battalions, as did the
Manchester Regiment, while the Middlesex Regiment raised
46. In typically idiosyncratic British fashion the numbering
of battalions can be confusing. The 1st Battalion of the King's
Own is obvious. The 1st/5th Battalion the King's Own is
the 1st Battalion of the 5th Territorial Army Battalion of the
King's Own, having hived off several battalions. The Australian
infantry battalions were numbered (1st Battalion, 2nd Battalion
etc.), as were the Canadian infantry. Although the Canadians
also raised two named regiments in the British fashion: The
Royal Canadian Regiment, and Princess Patricia's Canadian
Light Infantry, as well as adding titles in brackets to some of the
numbered battalions: e.g. 42nd (Royal Highlanders of Canada).
The New Zealanders gave their infantry battalions city names:
1st Wellington, 2nd Canterbury. They also raised a regiment
called the Rifle Brigade of three battalions. The South Africans
had numbered battalions, but like the Canadians, sometimes
added titles in brackets such as South African Scottish.

RFC – Royal Flying Corps, formed on 13 May 1912 to carry
out reconnaissance tasks for the Army.

RNAS – Royal Naval Air Service. The first naval officers
learned to fly in the spring of 1911. The RNAS was originally
the Naval Wing of the Royal Flying Corps (RFC) and its six
pilots appeared as such in the 1912 Army List. The Admiralty
rightly decided that it was not going to have policy matters
for its aviation wing decided by the RFC. By 1914, the Naval
Wing was firmly the RNAS and the modern Fleet Air Arm
celebrates that as its birth year. The RNAS experimented with
all types of aircraft, refusing to confine its purchases to the Royal
Aircraft Factory, or to ban monoplanes, which the RFC had
done on grounds of safety. By the outbreak of war the RNAS
had notched up several British aviation "firsts": flying off an
aircraft from a ship; the use of sea-planes to land on and take-off
from water; flying across country by night; flying in formation;
bomb-dropping; attacking other aircraft; and experimenting
with wireless. Meanwhile the RFC saw its role as solely
reconnaissance – that is until experience in the first few weeks of
the First World War opened up other roles.

INDEX

(page numbers in **bold** type refer to main entries; *italic* type refers to photographs and captions; ***bold italic*** type refers to maps)

Advance Hindenburg System 207
aircraft *see* by name
Aire Aerodrome *122–3*
airships *57, 60*, 61, *61*, 62, 69, *246–7*
Aisne, Battles of the *36, 37, 39, 42, 44*
Albert, Battle of **184–9**
Albert, King 201
Allen, George H. *15*
Allenby, Gen. Sir Edmund ("the Bull") 82, *82*, 83–7, 88, 163–5
Allied Supreme War Council 35
Alpine Corps 35
Alpini (Italy) *70–1, 73*
American Army 15, *112–13, 114, 115, 148*, 149, *149*, ***152***, *154, 155, 192, 193, 194–5, 196*, 197, 217, *218, 219*, 220–1, 242
American Expeditionary Force (AEF) 37, 149, 154
Amethyst, HMS 49
Amiens, Battle of 32, **118–47**, ***124, 126, 127***, 128, 129, *138*, 139, *144–5, 146–7*, ***152***, 185, *204*
Amiens–Roye road 139, *140*
Arc de Triomphe *248–9*
Argonne offensive ***190***, **190–7**, ***193***, 197, *216*, 217, 220–1, 225
Argus, HMS 62
Armentières 29, *31, 34, 35*, 187
Armistice 9, 165–7, **236–41**, *237, 238, 239, 241*
terms of 239
Army Group Boroevic (Austro-Hungary) 73, *74*
Army Group Conrad (Austro-Hungary) 73, *74*
Arnold, Lt Clement

Broomhall *135*, 136
Aulnoye 240
Aulnoye–Le Quesnoy railway *234–5*
Australian and New Zealand Mounted Division 83
Australian Corps 105, 121, 122, 136, *136–7, 142, 143*, 185, 207, *210–11*, 213
Australian Light Horse 85, *85*, 135, *163*
Austro-Hungarian Army 73, *74*, 75, 76–7, 179, *180–1*
Austro-Hungarian Empire 73, 75

"backing into the limelight" 84
Bailleul *31*, 32, *33*
Baku oil-fields 18
Balkans **168–75**, *170, 172, 173, 174–5*
Barry, 2nd Lt P.R.J. *239*
Basra 81
Batoum oil-fields 18
Battle Cruiser Fleet (BCF) (Britain) 244
"beaten zone" 135
Beatty, ADM Sir David 242, 244, *244*
Beersheba, Battle of *85*, 85, *86–7*
Belgian Army 201
Belleau Wood 44
Bellenglise 213
Béthune 29
Big Red One 44, 149
"bird cage" *109*
'birdcage' defence *169*
Birdwood, Gen. Sir William 231
Bishop, William 65, 68
"bite and hold" attacks 121
Black Watch *166–7*
Blanc Mont Ridge **216–21**, *218*
blitzkrieg 225
Blücher-Yorck Offensive *20, 42*
Boelcke, Oswald 68
Bois de Gattigny 225
Bois de la Vipère 217, *218*
Bois de Reims *97, 98*
Bojna, Svetozar Boroevic von

73, 76
Boxer Rebellion 49, 244
Braithwaite, Lt-Gen. Sir Walter 213
Bray–Corbie road 126
Breslau, SMS 61
Brest-Litovsk, Treaty of **14–19**
British Expeditionary Force (BEF) 10, 22, 25, 32, 35, 69, 100, 109, *116–17*, 119, *119*, 121, 185, 201, 223, 225, 231, 237, 242
GHQ 18
British Indian Army 81
British Official History 21, 129, 139, 143
Bruges 49
Brutinel, Brig. Gen. Raymond 139–40
Buckingham Palace *240*
Bulfin, Lt-Gen. Edward Stanislaus 82, 161
Burma 121
Bushell, Lt-Col. Christopher 126
"butcher's bill" 231
Byng, Gen. Sir Julian 21, 185

C3, HMS 52
Cadorna, Gen. Luigi 73, *76*, 179
Caëstre 29, *31*
Cambrai, Battles of **222–7**, *222, 223, 224, 225, 226–7*
Cameronians, First Battle of the 202
Campanula, HMS 58
Campbell, Brig. J. V. 213, *214*
Canadian Cavalry Brigade 139, 225
Canadian Corps 119, *140*, 185, 187, 201
Canadian Highlanders 140
Canadian Horse Artillery 225
Canadian Motor Machine Gun Brigades 139
Canadian Scottish 141, *202*
Canal du Nord **198–9**, *200*, **201–5**, *201, 202, 204, 205*
Cantigny 44
Cape Bon 61

Caporetto, Battle of 10, 73, *73, 75, 76*, 179
Carden, VADM Sackville 49
Cardiff, HMS 242
Carpenter, Capt. 52
Cassel 35
Cavalry Corps 225
Cavalry Corps (Britain) 119
Cavan, Earl of 179
Central Powers 15, 75
Chamber of Deputies 9
Champagne 38, 171, **216–21**
Charleroi, Battle of 100
Château-Thierry 38, *39*, 44, 45
Chauvel, Lt-Gen. Sir Henry 82, *85*, 161
Chemin des Dames 9, *37*, 38, *39*
Chetwode, Lt-Gen. Sir Philip 82
Chipilly spur 125, 126, *144–5*
Churchill, Winston 9, 81, *230, 231*, 244
Clemenceau, Georges ("Tiger") *7, 8*, 9, *9*, 26, 32, *32*, 245
Coates, John 144
Cockerill-Sambre steelworks *232*
conscription 35, 244
Constantine, King 168
Constantinople 61
convoys, introduction of 49, 60
Culley, Lt Stuart 61, 62, *62–3*
Currie, Lt-Gen. Sir Arthur 120, *120*, 139, 185, 187, 201
Cuxhaven Raid 61

Daffodil *46–7*, 49, *50–3*
Damascus 163, *163, 164*, 165
Dardanelles campaign 49
"death ride" 238
Debeney, Gen. Marie-Eugène *110, 111*
Dennis, Peter 144
Derfflinger, SMS *246–7*
Desert Mounted Corps (Britain) 82, *85, 164*, 165
Diaz, Gen. Armando 73, *76*,

77, 177, 179, *179*
directive particulière 111
dogfights 68
Dogger Bank, Battle of 61, 244
Dönitz, Karl 58
"dope" 68
"doughboys" 149
Doullens meeting 22
Dover Patrol (Britain) 49
Downes, Lt Rupert *91*
Dresden 172
Dreyfus, Capt. Alfred 32
Drocourt–Quéant position 187
Duke of Cornwall's Light Infantry *226–7*

Egyptian Expeditionary Force (EEF) 82, *162*, 163
Eighteenth Army (Germany) 21, 22, *39*, *43*, 44, *124*, *186*
Eighth Army (France) *152*
Eighth Army (Germany) 19, *162*
Eighth Army (Italy) *74*, 177, 179
Eighth Army (Turkey) 165
8th Submarine Flotilla (Britain) 49
Eisenhower, 10
El Arish 83
Eleventh Army (Germany) *74*
11th Battalion, Argyll and Sutherland Highlanders (Britain) *32*, *33*
11th Cyclist Battalion (Britain) 30
Emir Faisal 84
Emperor's Battle 21
Entente Allies 11, 73, 114, 165, 177, 245
Esdraelon, Plain of 161
Espèrey, Gen. Louis Franchet d' 171, *171*, 172
Essen Hill 217
Essex Regiment (Britain) 126
Estonia, occupation of 15

F.2A flying boats 58
Falkenhayn, Gen. Erich von 171
Falkenhayn, FM Erich von 11, *19*
Fayolle, Gen. Émile *110*, *111*
F.E.2b *122–3*
Ferdinand, Crown Prince, Franz 75
Festubert, Battles of *204*
Fifth Army (Austria) 179

Fifth Army (Britain) 21, 22, *23*, *39*, 121, 225, *230*, 231, *231*
Fifth Army (France) *99*, 171
Fifth Army (Germany) *191*, *193*
Fifth Army (Italy) 76
5th Marine Regiment (US) 153–4
50th Division 30
51st Division 30
56 Squadron RFC (Britain) *65*, 67
First Army (Britain) 185, *186*, 187, 201, 224, 231, 233
First Army (France) *43*, 114, *124*, *127*, *186*, *187*, 224, 231
First Army (Germany) *39*, *99*
First Army (Italy) *74*
First Army (US) 149, *152*, 154, 192, 225
1st Australian Division 30, 119, 207
1st Battalion Irish Guards *239*
1st Division (US) 44, 149
First World War 242
  air campaigns 68, 69
  "an all arms battle" 94
  America enters *112–13*, 149
  attack formations *134*
  casualties 22, 35, 44, 52, 77, 83, 84, *85*, 109, 147, 172, 223
  cause of 75, 238
  end of **236–41**, *236*, *237*, *238*, *239*, *240*, *241*
  final Australian ground action 209
  Germany's expansionist intentions justify 38
  instigators 75
  largest tank battle 144
  last weeks of **230–5**
  lead up to 32, 73, 204
  museum *see* Imperial War Museum
  naval campaigns 49, 57, 61
  official end of 243
  outbreak of 49, 84, 120, 169
  POWs *108–9*, *130–1*, *132*, *133*, *136–7*, *156–7*, 171, *180–1*, *182–3*, 185, *210–11*, *212*, *213*, 223, *226–7*
  reconnaissance 65
  small battles 109
  submarine warfare **56–63**, *56*, *57*

terms of Armistice 239
trench warfare *187*, *218*, 219
turning point 114
US enters 38, 44
winning 245
Fismes *42*
Flanders 24, 32, 35, 38, 44, 119, **201–5**, *203*
Flanders Group 201
"Flying Circus" 65, 68
Foch, Mar. Ferdinand 9, 10, *10*, 30, 32, 35, *35*, 38, 44, 77, 97, *110*, 111, *111*, 115, 147, 177, *237*, 238, 242
Fokker DR-1 *66–7*, 68
Fort Garry Horse 225
Forward Zone 21
Fourth Army (Britain) *39*, 105, *110*, 111, *111*, *113*, 121, *124*, *127*, 185, *186*, 217, 223, 224, 225, 231, 233
Fourth Army (France) *99*, *152*, 192, *193*, 217, 225
Fourth Army (Germany) 30, *31*, 144, *162*
Fourth Army (Italy) *74*, 177, 179
Fourth Army (Turkey) 165
4th Battalion Royal Marines (4 RM) (Britain) 50, 52
4th Battle Squadron (Britain) 49
4th Guards Brigade (Britain) 30
4th Marine Brigade (US) 153
France, Second Empire 32
Franco-Prussian War *35*, 242
French, FM Sir John 22, 25
French Army 9, 21, *23*, 98, *237*
French Forward Zone 98
Furious, HMS *57*, *59*, 62

Galicia campaign 75, 76
Gallipoli 81, 106, 168, 171
Gaza 83, *85*, 88, *164*
George Barrie's Sons *15*
George V *110*, 111, *142*, *143*, *150*, *151*
German Air Force 98
German Alpine Corps 35
German Army 11, 115, *232*, *236*, *237*, *242*, *243*
German Army Air Service 68
Germany:
  April offensive 11
  last offensive *99*
  March offensive 11, 52, 119

May/June Offensive **36–45**
Russia cedes territory to *14*,
15–16, *15*
Second Army 19
Spring Offensive *20*, **20–35**
Treaty of Versailles **242–9**
victory myth *243*
GHQ Intelligence 18
Gibbs, Cdr Valentine 52
Goeben, SMS 61
Gordon Highlanders *180–1*
Gough, Lt-Gen. Sir Hubert 22, *22*, *23*, 121
Gourand, Gen. Henri 217
Grand Fleet (Britain/US) 238, 242, 244
Grant, Brig. Gen. *85*
Great War *see* First World War
The Great War (Allen) *15*
Grey, Sir Edward 242
Guards Division (Britain) 201

Habsburg Empire 75, 76, 77
Haig, FM Sir Douglas *6*, *8*, *9*, 10, 22, 25, *25*, 30–2, 44, *82*, 109, *110*, 111, 114, 121, *146–7*, 147, 185, *204*
Handley Page *90*, *91*, *94–5*
Harwich 49
Harwich Force 61
Hasa Su *82–3*
Haverskerque *30*
Havre *112–13*
Hazebrouck 30, *31*
Heinl, Robert Debs Jr 154
Hejaz 84
Helgoland, Battle of 244
Heligoland Bight, Battle 49
High Seas Fleet (German) 238, 242, *246–7*
Hindenburg Line 153, 185, 187, *206*, **207–11**, *207*, *208*, *209*, 213
Hindenburg, FM Paul von 11, *11*, 19, *19*, 114, 237
Hindenburg, SMS *246–7*
Hipper, ADM Franz von 238
Hitler, Adolf 11, 18, 237, 245
Hollyhock, HMS 58, 61
Horne, Gen. Sir Henry 185, 204, *204*
Horne, Lt Harold 239
Hötzendorf, FM Conrad von 73, 75, *75*
Hundred Days, Battle of the 125
hydrophones 56

Hymn 227, A&M, v.7 61

I Corps (France) 171
I Corps (US) *152*
II Col Corps (France) *152*
II Corps (US) 209
III Corps (Britain) 119, 121,
    125, 126, *128*, 129, *129*,
    136, 143, 207
Imperial War Museum *63*
Independence Day 108
Independent Force 139, 140,
    140
Infantry Brigade (Britain)
    213, *214*
interwar years 84
Iris 50
Isonzo, Battles of the 73,
    74, 76
Italian Army *72*, 73, *73*, **74**,
    75, 77, *78–9*, *176*, *177*,
    178, 179
Italo-Turkish War 179
IV Corps (US) *152*
IX Corps (Britain) *42*, 207,
    209, 213

Jack, Brig. Gen. J. L. 202
Jagdgeschwader 1 (JG1)
    (Germany) 68
Jagdstaffel 2 (Germany) 68
Jellicoe, ADM Sir John 244
Jerusalem 163
Joffre, Gen. Joseph 171
Juno, HMS 244
Jutland, Battle of 243, 244

Kaiserschlacht 21
Karl, Emperor 75
Kemmel, Mt *31*, 35, *40–1*
Keyes, VADM Roger 49–50,
    49
Kiev:
    capture of 15
    occupation of *15*, *18*
King Edward's Horse (Britain)
    30
King's Own Yorkshire Light
    Infantry *96*, *97*, *98*
Kitchener, Lord *76*
Kosturino 172
Kut-al-Amara 81

L-35 61
Labour Corps (Britain) 32
Lacy, Charles de *49*
Lanrezac, Gen. Charles 171
Lawrence, T. E. 84, *84*, 88,
    163, **164**
Le Cateau **222–7**, 225
Le Hamel, Battle of **104–9**,

104, *105*, *106*, **107**, *108–9*,
    121
Le Quesnel 141, *141*
Lebensraum 18
Lejeune, Maj.-Gen. John A.
    153, 197, 217, 219, *219*
Lenin, Vladimir 15, 16, 17
Lille *228–9*, **230–5**, *230*, *231*
Liverpool Regiment *233*
"living space" 18
Livonia, occupation of 15
Lloyd George, David 9, *10*,
    22, 25, 32, *82*, 83, 167,
    245
    "Welsh Wizard" sobriquet
    10
London, Secret Treaty of
    (1915) 73
Louis XIV 242
Lowland Scots *158–9*, *161*
Loyal North Lancashire
    Regiment *224*, *225*
Ludendorff, Gen. Erich von
    11, *11*, 18, 19, *19*, 22–4,
    37–8, 44, 97, 100, 114–15,
    141, 147, 172, 233, 237
    offensives "talked up" by 45
Lurcher, HMS 49
Lys, Battle of the *28*, *29*, 30,
    31, 32, *33*, 35

MacArthur, Maj.-Gen.
    Douglas 197
McCudden, James 65, 67, *67*,
    68, 69
Machine Gun Corps (MGC)
    (Britain) *30*
Manchester Regiment *222*,
    223
Mangin, Gen. Charles 98,
    100, *100*
Mannock, Maj. Edward
    ("Mick") 65, *65*, 68, 69
Marcoing Line 201
Marne, Battles of the **96–103**,
    101, *102–3*, 171
Marquion Line 201
Marshall, Col. George C. 192,
    197, *197*
Maubeuge 240
Maude, Lt-Gen. Frederick
    Stanley 81
Megiddo, Battle of **161–7**,
    161, **162**, *166–7*
Melbourne University
    Company 106
Merchant Navy (MN) 60
Mesopotamia 81–3, *160*, *161*,
    163, 165, 167
"Mespot" 81
Messerschmitt Bf 109 *165*

Messines Ridge 187
Metcalf, LCpl William 187
Meuse attack **190**, *190–7*,
    193
Mézières 191
Middle East **80**, *80–7*, 167
"military sin" 24
Mole *46–7*, 49, *50–2*
Moltke, SMS *246–7*
Monash, Lt-Gen. John 105,
    106, *106*, 108, 121–2, *142*,
    143, 185, 207, 213
Monchy-le-Preux *188–9*
Mont des Cats 35
Mont St Quentin 185
Montdidier *43*, 44, *44*
Montdidier-Noyon sector *37*
Monte Grappa 179
Monte Nero *72*, *73*
Montfaucon *191*, 192, **192**,
    197
Moro insurrection 38
Morvada, HMS 61
Muckydonia *174–5*
Mules 119, *172*, *173*, 192
Murray, Gen. Sir Archibald 83

Napoleon III 32
Neuve Chapelle 30, **31**
Nineteenth Army (Germany)
    152
Ninth Army (Germany) **99**,
    144, **186**
Ninth Army (Italy) *74*, 77
Nivelle, Gen. Robert 9, 10,
    100, 171
Nova Scotia Highlanders
    146–7
Noyon *43*, 44, *44*, 97
nuclear weapons 69
Number 22 Squadron
    (Britain) *120*
Number 3 Squadron RFC
    67

October Revolution 17
Odessa:
    capture of 15
    occupation of 18
O'Hare, Pte Arthur John *233*
113th (Jat) Regiment *160*,
    161
153rd Regiment 207
165th Infantry Regiment
    (Britain) 153
Operations:
    Blücher-York **20**
    Georgette **20**, **28–35**, *30*
    Gneisenau **20**
    Marne-Reims **20**
    Michael **20**, **20–7**, **23**, 30,

35, 69
Orlando, Vittorio 245
Ostend Raid 49, *50–2*, 61
"other side of the hill" 114
Ottoman Empire **80**, 84

Padua 73
Paget, Capt. *A. W.L. 239*
Palestine 83–7, *163–7*, **164**
Pas-de-Calais 26
Passchendaele 22, 30, 106,
    120, 139, 201
Péronne *24*, 185
Pershing, Maj.-Gen. John 9,
    37, 38, *38*, *150*, *151*, 153,
    192, 197
Pétain, Gen. Philippe 9, 22,
    26, *26*, 32, *110*, *111*
Piave, Battle of the 10, **72–9**,
    74, *75*, 77, *78–9*, 177, 179
Picardy 30, 32
Plumer, Gen. Sir Herbert
    30, 231
Pont-Arcy *42*
Prémont *222*, *223*
Prussian Guard 11, 185

Quennemont Farm 207
"quiet sector" 38

railways *118*, *119*
Rapallo meeting 10
Rawlinson, Gen. Sir Henry
    22, 105, *110*, *111*, 121,
    121, 125, 147, 185, 207
Red Army 17
Redoubt, HMS 61
"refusing a flank" 220
Reims **20**, **39**, 44, 45
Ribbans, Pte Christopher 136
Richthofen, Manfred von
    ("Red Baron") 65, 68,
    68, 69
Ridge Line 207
Robeck, VADM John de 49
Robertson, Gen. Sir William
    9, 10, *10*
"Rock of the Marne" 45
Romania, occupation of 18
Roosevelt, Franklin D. 197
Rothermere, Lord 69
Royal Air Force (RAF) 93,
    108, 121, *122–3*, 125, 144,
    202, 232
    "Independent Force" 69
Royal Artillery (RA) *204*
Royal Engineers (RE) 67, 68,
    200, *201*, 213, *214*
Royal Field Artillery *223*
Royal Flying Corps (RFC)
    64–9, 67, 69, *69*

Royal Marine Artillery (RMA) 50
Royal Marine Brigade 223
Royal Marine Light Infantry 239
Royal Marines Light Infantry (RMLI) 50
Royal Navy Air Service (RNAS) 61, *61*, 62, *62–3*, 69
Royal Navy (RN) 10, 49, 61, 81, 100, 242
Rupprecht, Crown Prince 231
Russia, Hitler invades 18

St Étienne 220
Saint-Floris *28*, *29*, *32*, *33*
St Mihiel *148*, *149*, *149*, *153*, *154*, *155*, *156–7*, 197
St Quentin 22, *26–7*, 185, 191, 207, **210** *15*, 216
Salonika, gardeners of 172
Sambre 231, *232*, 233, *234*, *234–5*, 240
Sarrail, Gen. Maurice *168*, *169*
Scarpe, Battle of the **184–9**, *184*, 185, **186**
SE5A *64*, *65*, 67
Seaforth Highlanders *184*, *185*
Second Army (Britain) 185, 201, 202, 225, 231
Second Army (Germany) 21, 22, ***31***, ***124***, ***127***, ***186***
Second Boer War 22, 121
2nd Cavalry Division (Britain) 22, *141*
2nd Division (US) 153
2nd Infantry Brigade (Canada) 120
2nd Infantry Division (US) 44
2nd West Yorkshires 202
Second World War 10, 49, *57*, 92,   94, 121, 135–6, 245
lead up to 197
naval campaigns *57*, 58
outbreak of 57
strategic bombing 69
tank warfare 144
Seely, John 22
"self determined areas" **14**, *15*
Selle 231
Selle, Battle of the 232
Serbia, Central Powers invade 75
Seven Pillars of Wisdom (Lawrence) 88
Seventeenth Army (Germany) 21, 22, ***186***

Seventh Army (Germany) ***39***, *43*, 44, ***99***, ***162***, ***186***
Seventh Army (Turkey) 165
7th Queens (Royal West Surrey) 126
7th Royal West Kents 126, 129
Seydlitz, SMS *246–7*
Sharif Hussein 84
Sinai 83
Sinclair-Maclagan, Maj.-Gen. Ewen 105, ***107***
6th American Battle Squadron 242
Sixth Army (Austria) 179
Sixth Army (France) ***99***
Sixth Army (Germany) 29, 30, ***74***, ***186***
Sixth Army (Italy) ***74***
Soissons ***39***, 45, 100, 154
Sokolnikov, Grigori 16–17
Soldiers of the Sea (Heinl) 154
Somme, Battle of the 22, 44, 92, 105, 120, 121, 125–6, 143–4,   *204*
Somme-Py 217
Sopwith Camel 61, 62, *62–3*, 68
"SOS target" 121
South African Brigade 225
Spanish–American War 38, 219
Staffordshire Brigade 213, 214, *214*
Stalin, Joseph 17
stormtroopers *12–13*, *15*, 24, *37*
Strathcona, Lord 225
submarine warfare 114
Sudan Campaign 244
Suez Canal *80*, 83, *204*
Supreme War Council, setting up of 10

Tank Corps (Britain) *128*, *129*, *209*
tanks 89–90, *91*, *92*, *93*, *132*, *133*, *212*, *213*
A7V (German) *24*, *25*
"brewed up" 144
FT-17 *196*
Mark II (Britain) 108
Mark IV (Britain) *24*
Mark V (Britain) 92, 108, *128*, *129*, 133, *209*
Medium Mark A (Britain) 92
"Musical Box" *135*, 136
Renault *114*, *153*, *196*, 197
Whippet 92, *92*, 136
Tardenois, Battle of *97*, *98*

Tenth Army (Britain) ***39***
Tenth Army (France) ***43***, 100, ***186***
Tenth Army (Italy) 177, 179
Terschelling 61
Third Army (Britain) 21, 22, *82*, 147, 185, ***186***, 201, 223, 224, 231–2, 233, 240
Third Army (France) ***43***, ***186***
Third Army (Germany) ***99***
Third Army (Italy) ***74***
3rd Battalion The 3rd Gurkha Rifles (Britain) *81*
3rd Division (US) 45
3rd Infantry Division (US) 44
13th Hussars (Britain) *82–3*
38th Infantry Regiment (US) 45
Thompson, Capt. Arnold 240
Tønder *57*
Townshend, Maj.-Gen. Sir Charles Vere Ferrers 81
trench warfare *21*
Trenchard, Maj.-Gen. Sir Hugh ("Boom") 69, *69*
Trento 179
Trieste 73, 177, 179
Triple Alliance 73
Trotsky, Leon 15, 16, *16–17*
death of 17
Turkish Navy 61
Twelfth Army (Italy) 177, 179
29th Battalion (Australia) *91*
Tyrwhitt, RAdm Reginald 61, *61*

U-boats 49, 52, 69, 242
Ukraine, occupation of 15, 18
US Autocar Company *140*
US Marine Brigade 100
US Marine Corps (USMC) 197, 219
USAAF 69

V Corps (Britain) 240
V Corps (US) ***152***
Val d'Assa *178*
Varennes *220–1*
Veracruz, Battle of 219
Verdun, Battle of 26, 100, 171, *191*
Verona 73
Versailles, Treaty of **242–9**, *245*
victory celebrations *240*, *241*, *248–9*
Villa, Pancho 38
Villers-Bretonneux 35
Vimy Ridge 120, *204*
Vindictive, HMS *46–7*, *48*, *49*, 50–2, *50*, *54–5*

Virginia Military Institute 197
Vittorio Veneto, Battle of 176–81, *176*, *177*, *182–3*, *185*
Von Der Tann, SMS *246–7*

War Council (Britain) 83
War Office (Britain) 84
Wemyss, ADM Sir Rosslyn *237*
Weygand, Gen. Maxime *110*, *111*, *111*, *237*
Wheeler-Bennett, Sir John 15
Wilhelm II 11, *11*, *19*, 147, *191*, 233
abdication 238, *238*
Wilhelm, King 242
Wilson, Henry 10
Wilson, Woodrow 177, 244, 245
"win or bust" strategy 19
World War I *see* First World War
World War II *see* Second World War

XI Corps (Britain) *230*, *231*, *233*
XI Corps (France) 220
XI Corps School (Britain) *115*
XV Corps (Britain) *204*
XVII Corps (Britain) 223
XIX Corps 121
XX Corps (Britain) 82
XX Corps (EEF) 165
XX Corps (France) 100
XXI Corps (Britain) 82

Yilderim Army Group ***162***, 165
Ypres ***31***, 35
First Battle of 201
Fourth Battle of 30
Second Battle of 120
Third Battle of 22, 30, 106, 120, 139, 201
Yser position ***31***, 35

Zeebrugge Raid *46–7*, **48–55**, *49*, *49*, 50–2, *50*, *55*, 61
Zeppelin activity *57*, 61, 62, 69
0/400 bomber 90, *91*
Zero Hour 108, 125, 133, 135, 139

CREDITS

The majority of the photographs reproduced in the book have been taken from the collection of the Imperial War Museums, London.

The reference numbers for each of the photographs are listed below.

6-7. Q 9553, 8. Q 7629, 11. Q 23746, 12-13. Q 47997, 17. Q 23903, 18. Q 86876, 19. Q 23746, 22. Q 35825D, 24. Q 10838, 28. Q 7882, 29. Q 6570, 30. Q 6571, 33. (top) Q 6613, 36. Q 50512, 37. Q 55008, 39. Q 47999, 42. (top) Q 55010, (bottom) Q 55013, 44-45. Q 55322, 46-47. ART 871, 48. Q 20849, 49. ART 1324, 50. (left) Q 36379, 52. Q 50282, 56. Q 18630, 57. Q 19557, 58. Q 27501, 60. Q 27433, 62-63. Q 27511, 65. Q 73408, 67. HU 71314, 68. Q 58028, 70-71. Q 115126, 72. Q 65158, 75. (top) Q 65091, 76. (top) Q 65097, 81. Q 12937, 82. (top) Q 82969, 82-83. Q 24707, 84. (top) Q 24168, (bottom) Q 73534, 86-87. Q 50576, 88-89. Q 14508, 90. Q 12035, 91. E (AUS) 2790, 92. Q 64484, 93. Q 48200, 94-95. Q 68141, 96. Q 11113, 97. Q 55349, 98. Q 11107, 102-103. Q 56487, 110. Q 9251, 112. Q 6850, 115. Q 222, 116-117. Q 70709, 118. Q 8860, 119. (top) Q 12058, 122-123. Q 11958, 126. CO 3007, 128. Q 9263, 140. CO 3085, 141. Q 8198, 143. Q 9242, 144-145. Q 9191, 146-147. CO 3015, 150-151. Q 9259, 158-159. Q 32740, 160. Q. 24791, 161. Q 12977, 163. Q 12355, 165. Q 24781, 166-167. Q 12485, 168. Q 32203, 169. Q 31840, 170. Q 42377, 172. Q 31798, 173. Q 32337, 174-175. Q 32682, 176. Q 25946, 177. Q 26514, 178. Q 25950, 180-181. Q 26693, 182-183. Q 86118, 184. Q 7013, 187. Q 72619, 188-189. Q 7028, 191. Q 49849, 192. Q 85383, 193. Q 70736, 194-195. Q 108353, 196. (top) Q 58691, (bottom) Q 69946, 198-199. Q 9633, 200. Q 9344, 202. CO 3289, 204. (top) Q 9327, (bottom) Q 9018, 205. Q 9325, 206. E (AUS) 3260, 209. Q 9365, 210-211. E (AUS) 3274, 212. Q 9370, 222. Q 7113, 223. Q 78754, 224. Q 11366, 225. Q 11367, 226-227. Q 11435, 228-229. Q 9629, 230. Q 11423, 232. Q 69980, 233. Q 9579, 234. Q 47076, 237. Q 43225, 238. Q (left) 47933, 239. Q 3365, 241. Q 69030, 244. SP 3129, 245. Q 48222, 246. Q 20614, 248-249. Q 81860

Photographs kindly supplied by sources outside the archives of the Imperial War Museums.

10. Chronicle/Alamy Stock Photo, 15. AKG-Images, 16-17. Public Domain, 21. Ullstein bild via Getty Images, 25. (top) Harlingue/Roger Viollet/Getty Images (bottom) Ullstein bild via Getty Images, 26. The Print Collector/Getty Images, 26-27. Ullstein bild via Getty Images, 32. Bettmann/Getty Images, 33. (bottom) Paul Popper/Popperfoto/Getty Images, 34. (top) dpa picture alliance /Alamy Stock Photo, (bottom) Hulton Archive/Getty Images, 35. Peter Stone Archive/Alamy Stock Photo, 38. Bettmann/Getty Images, 50. NMRN, 51. Author Collection, 53. © Royal Marines Museum, 54-55. Trinity Mirror/Mirrorpix/Alamy Stock Photo, 59. Hulton Archive/Getty Images, 61. Universal History Archive/Getty Images, 64. Chronicle/Alamy Stock Photo, 66-67. Hulton Archive/Getty Images, 69. Spencer Arnold/Hulton Archive/Getty Images, 75. & 76. (bottom) DeAgostini/Getty Images, 77. Granger Historical Picture Archive/Alamy Stock Photo, 78-79. Chronicle/Alamy Stock Photo, 100. Public Domain, 104. AWM E02669, 105. AWM E02665, 106. (top) AWM E02694, (bottom) Bettmann/Getty Images, 108-109. AWM E02698, 114. Chronicle/Alamy Stock Photo, 120. (bottom) City of Vancouver Archives, 121. Ullstein bild via Getty Images, 129. AWM E03884, 130-131. AWM E03017, 132-137. Chronicle/Alamy Stock Photo, 138. Topfoto.co.uk, 148. Photo12/UIG via Getty Images, 153. PhotoQuest/Getty Images, 154. REX/Shutterstock, 155. Granger Historical Picture Archive/Alamy Stock Photo, 156-157. Topfoto.co.uk, 171. Henri Martinie/Roger Viollet/Getty Images, 179. DeAgostini/ Getty Images, 197. PhotoQuest/Getty Images, 214-215. Three Lions/ Getty Images, 216. Public Domain, 218. Fotosearch/Getty Images, 219. (top) Library of Congress, (bottom) Science History Images/Alamy Stock Photo, 220-221. The Print Collector/Getty Images, 236. © SZ Photo/ Bridgeman Images, 240. Universal History Archive/UIG via Getty Images, 242. Historica Graphica Collection/Heritage Images/Getty Images

Every effort has been made to acknowledge correctly and contact the source and/or copyright holder of each photograph and Carlton Books Limited apologises for any unintentional errors or omissions, which will be corrected in future editions of this book.